EARTH, WATER, AND SKY

Number Forty-one
The Corrie Herring Hooks Series

PAUL A. JOHNSGARD

Earth,

A Water, and

NATURALIST'S Sky

STORIES AND SKETCHES

UNIVERSITY OF TEXAS PRESS AUSTIN

For information regarding previous publication of these essays, see pages 161–162.

Requests for permission to reproduce material from this work should be sent to Permissions, University of Texas Press, P.O. Box 7819, Austin, TX 78713-7819.

♾ The paper used in this book meets the minimum requirements of ANSI/NISO Z39.48-1992 (R1997) (Permanence of Paper).

LIBRARY OF CONGRESS CATALOGING-IN-PUBLICATION DATA

Johnsgard, Paul A.
    Earth, water, and sky : a naturalist's stories and sketches / by Paul A. Johnsgard. — 1st ed.
            p.   cm. — (Corrie Herring Hooks series ; no. 41)
    Includes bibliographical references (p.   ) and index.
    ISBN 0-292-74058-1 (cloth : alk. paper). —
    ISBN 0-292-74059-X (pbk. : alk paper)
    1. Birds.   I. Title.   II. Series.
QL673.J625   1999
598—dc21   98-49419

IN MEMORY OF MY FIRST-GRADE TEACHER

Hazel Bilstad

WHO GAVE ME A PRECIOUS GIFT, BUT DIDN'T
LIVE LONG ENOUGH FOR ME TO REPAY HER

Contents

Preface *xi*

I. *Earth* STRAY FEATHERS IN THE DUST *1*

Sacred Places and the Voices of Ancestors *3*

Dawn Rendezvous on the Lek *6*

The Elusive Tree Quails of Mexico *16*

Quail Music *26*

On Display: The Pheasants *33*

Bustards: Stalkers of the Dry Plains *44*

Glittering Garments of the Rainbow *50*

II. *Water* A RIVER OF TIME *61*

Adrift in Time on the Niobrara River *63*

The Evolution of Duck Courtship *66*

The Elusive Musk Duck *79*

86 The Unlikely Ruddy Duck

92 Torrent Ducks of the Andes

101 Seabirds of the Pribilofs

109 III. *Sky* MIGRATIONS OF THE IMAGINATION

110 The Gifts of the Cranes

115 Flight of the Sea Ducks

123 The Triumphant Trumpeters

130 The 6,000-mile Odyssey of a Globe-trotting Bird

139 Where Have All the Curlews Gone?

147 The Geese from beyond the North Wind

159 Suggested Readings

161 Citations for Previously Published Articles

163 Index

List of Illustrations

Male Greater Prairie-Chicken in display 2

Sage Grouse in display 7

Adult Bearded Tree Quail 16

Male Gambel's Quail calling 27

Male Gray Peacock-Pheasant in frontal display 33

Male Australian Bustard performing balloon display 45

Female Calliope Hummingbird incubating 50

Long-billed Curlew calling in flight 62

Male North American Ruddy Duck in display 66

Social courtship by American Wigeon (A), Yellow-billed 69
Teal (B), Falcated Duck (C), and Mallard (D)

Social courtship by Surf Scoter (A), Common Eider (B), 74
Common Goldeneye (C), and Hooded Merganser (D)

Adult male Musk Duck chasing a diving beetle 78

Male North American Ruddy Duck performing 86
bubbling display to a female

92 Male Colombian Torrent Duck

100 Common Murre landing

110 Sandhill Crane calling

115 Male Spectacled Eider in flight

122 Trumpeter Swan in flight

130 American Golden-Plover chicks and eggs

138 Eskimo Curlew in flight

147 Snow Geese in flight

Preface

I WAS BORN IN 1931, IN A TINY, DUSTY VILLAGE IN eastern North Dakota, in the midst of the Great Depression. The village, Christine, then held fewer than a hundred people, mostly of Norwegian descent, and mostly of first- or second-generation Americans. It had a general store (owned and run by my grandfather), a grocery store, a barber shop, a filling station, a cafe, and a bar. The main street was a block long. There was also a train depot and a church, Norwegian Lutheran of course, that was just across the street from our little white house. Dad worked for his father in the general store, and Mother struggled at home with the problems of raising me and my two brothers (one three years older, one six years younger) on a tiny income. I remember the blistering hot summers, sitting by the dusty streets with nothing to do but watch grasshoppers, and trudging to school day after day in winter, often in subzero temperature.

We lived on the western edge of town, and to get to grade school meant walking the length of the town, crossing the railroad tracks, and then walking another few hundred yards (it seemed like miles during winter) along a dirt road leading to the brick schoolhouse well beyond the eastern limits of town. I believe there were only four teaching classrooms on the main floor of the school. The one I remember best had the first three grades in it (no kindergarten), and, since we left town when I was in the third grade, I never saw the others. The only decoration I remember on the classroom wall was a poster for Pepsodent toothpaste sternly advocating regular brushing. There was no library, but a large gymnasium was in the basement. There were four students in my first-grade class: two girls, another boy, and myself. Our teacher was Miss Hazel Bilstad, a person I remember as being wonderfully beautiful, and apparently quite new at teaching. I also remember that she sent me a picture postcard from Yellowstone Park the summer after first grade, which I cherished greatly. I was extremely shy in those years, and slightly speech-impaired, so I said very little. I was extremely fond of Miss Bilstad, and when I learned several years later that she had died of a brain tumor when only twenty-nine, I never fully recovered from that sadness.

The railroad tracks through town led north and south across the flat, treeless Red River Valley. It was planted to endless fields of spring wheat, but along the right-of-way there were still remnants of prairies, and associated prairie flowers. By the time I was five I would make regular walks out along the tracks, searching for wildflowers to bring home to Mother. I knew the names of only a few, but Mother's books helped. I was badly nearsighted, and had difficulty seeing and identifying birds at any distance. This being the Depression, the thought of being tested for glasses never occurred to anybody, and the nearest optometrist would have been in Fargo, 20 miles and in those days a virtual light-year away.

At some time during the period I was in first or second grade, Miss Bilstad recognized that I was fond of nature, and invited me to stop at her house and see a stuffed bird that she had. I had never seen a stuffed animal of any kind and was eager to do so. When I stopped, she led me to a bell jar, inside which was a mounted male Red-winged Blackbird. It was perched on a branch, with its wings spread enough to see its red epaulets. I was entranced; I had never seen anything so wonderful in my life. Even today, more than sixty years later, I can remember that moment of childhood epiphany.

It must have been at that moment that I became permanently hooked on birds. When I got home I asked Mother about using an antique brass telescope she had brought from her family's farm when she was married. It dated from the mid-1800s, and my great-grandfather had reportedly "liberated" it from the South during Sherman's infamous march through Georgia. It was big, heavy, and clumsy, with one cracked lens, but it was also miraculous. I still have this grand old telescope, and have recently determined that it only has a magnification of about three power and, as compared with modern optics, a very narrow field of view. I didn't own any other optical equipment until I received my first pair of binoculars, as a high school graduation gift.

Mother had been reared on a homestead farm and still had several books on birds and flowers dating from her childhood. These included a copy of Chester Reed's 1912 *Color Key to North American Birds,* which by then was in tatters, with most of its pages loose or even having fallen out. It had rather primitive color illustrations of hundreds of American birds, but at the time was the only thing of its kind available. It provided my first real guide to identifying birds. By 1934 Roger Peterson's first field guide had also been published, but I knew nothing of such things.

In 1939 my aunt sent me a most wonderful present for Christmas, a copy of J. J. Audubon's *Birds of America.* This book not only had great color illustrations of birds, but its fine plates also allowed me to identify many plants. I still possess and cherish it. The next spring, when I was still in third grade, we left Christine. Dad had gotten a job in Wahpeton, a much larger town south of Christine, with a wonderful public library. Among the library's treasures was a two-volume set of Thomas Roberts's *The Birds of Minnesota*, published in 1932. It had been judiciously placed on the reference shelf, where it could be read, but not checked out. That book became my guiding light, as it had wonderful paintings and accounts of all the species of Minnesota birds, the Wood Duck being my special favorite. I referred to it hundreds of times. After I became an adult and left Wahpeton for college, returning home only occasionally, I would always try to visit the library to make certain that this great reference was still safely there. About five years ago I noticed that, although several of my own titles were now listed in the card catalog, there was no trace of *The Birds of Minnesota*. My heart sank at learning this, but I hoped that perhaps it had been sold at a library sale to some young boy or girl who might treasure it even more than I.

As I write this, I am sitting in a cabin at Cedar Point Biological Station in southwestern Nebraska, where I have taught classes in ornithology nearly every year since 1977. Through my window I can look directly across a grassy ravine, where meadowlarks, Field Sparrows, and Lark Sparrows are now singing, toward the rocky slopes of a cedar-studded cliffside, where the occasional call of a Rock Wren can be heard. Farther up the ravine to my left I can just see the head of a box canyon, where a pair of Black-billed Magpies are nesting, and where the persistent calls of a Common Poorwill ring out like clockwork on most calm, moonlit nights. To my right, I easily scan nearby Keystone Lake, where on a small island near the middle of the lake, a handful of American White Pelicans resemble small white bandages pasted on a blue cloth field. Smaller, starlike white dots are produced by a scattering of Ring-billed Gulls, four Caspian Terns, and a lone Herring Gull. With the aid of a telescope nonbreeding Western Grebes can be seen bobbing on the lake, as can a few Great Blue Herons that are seemingly loitering along the far shoreline. Overhead there is only a scattering of cumulus clouds, but toward the lake I can see hundreds of busily foraging Cliff Swallows, and above the clifftops in the distance a few Turkey Vultures drift lazily in the wind. This glorious elemental mixture of earth, water, and sky is the home of nearly three hundred species of birds, and comprises one of my favorite places in the world. Here no radio stations blare out the most recent results of meaningless sports events, few newspapers ever manage to find their way to this outpost of civilization, and no traffic noises confound the senses. Instead the wind is the unquestioned dominating summer influence, the prairie grasses bend willingly and gracefully before it, and the leaves of the cottonwood trees convert its breezes into soft music.

Cedar Point in summer thus presents an idyllic scene, but these superficialities sometimes mask the realities of life and death that occur in the day-to-day struggles for existence among all the resident wildlife. Only a month ago a prolonged period of cold, rainy weather struck just after the Cliff Swallows had returned from their wintering grounds in South America, at a time when the birds were desperate for fresh insect food. The few insects that had already emerged suddenly disappeared, and the swallows died by the uncounted thousands. One of the Cedar Point researchers gathered up to 1,800 swallow carcasses in a short time. Even today, a month later, one can still see the dried-out corpses of swallows that froze or starved while huddling together for warmth in their last-year's adobe nests, their bodies still clinging to their nest interiors like victims of a genocidal slaughter. Similarly, a late-May snowstorm a few years ago literally knocked flocks of Cliff Swallows out of the sky; hundreds of weakened and dying birds could then be seen staggering along roadsides in a futile search for frozen insects. And yesterday my class and I came upon a dead Turkey Vulture lying at the base of an electric power pole; nothing in the past evolutionary history of vultures has warned the birds about the possible dangers of touching live electrical wires!

I can think of several reasons for anybody to begin studying or, at the very least, observing birds. First, it is both tremendously relaxing and yet simultaneously exciting to watch birds. It is relaxing in that familiar birds are much like old friends, each with its characteristic postures, expressions, and idiosyncrasies to watch for and enjoy. It is always fun to casually be able to say something like, "Watch the middle bird; it's getting ready to display," or, "Look at that goose family, it's just about ready to take off." Yet birds seen for the first time offer an exciting appeal and often provide the same mysterious attraction and desire to learn more as in the making of some new human acquaintances. Who cannot remember the first wild Wood Duck that he or she ever saw, or the first flock of Roseate Spoonbills? Then, there is the pure aesthetic appeal of birds; their shapes, colors, vocalization, and behaviors that somehow always seem "just right." While watching a particular bird I have often thought, "This is exactly the kind of animal I would have tried to invent, if I had been assigned to be a design engineer in a bird factory." From this initial appreciation comes a strong desire in many creative people to draw, paint, or photograph wild birds.

The aesthetic beauty of birds is often so great that many people can't dismiss the idea that some kind of creative mind must have been behind, for example, the stunning plumage and displays of a male Greater Bird of Paradise or a Rose-breasted Grosbeak, or the artistically perfect patterning on each of the body feathers of an Emperor Goose. Luckily, Charles Darwin provided us with a logical answer to the question of how birds (and humans) ever evolved a sense of aesthetic beauty. This brings us to another reason for watching birds: they have been so important in helping biologists understand such basic biological phenomena as territoriality, social dominance, pair bonding, and, perhaps most importantly, the processes by which species are formed. Regrettably, birds sometimes also show us how rapidly a species can disappear from the earth, which also may be a "natural" process, but is one that humans have greatly accelerated throughout the world.

Roger Tory Peterson, whose field guides have inspired and assisted millions of would-be bird-identifiers, has noted that birds are often highly sensitive bioindicators of subtle environmental changes. They typically respond dramatically to environmental changes, not only to such direct and obvious forces as the dramatic weather changes mentioned above, but also to such essentially invisible dangers as the slow but deadly insinuation of long-lasting pesticides into our environment during the 1950s and 1960s.

Roger Peterson has also observed that bird-watching (more accurately, birding) has in recent years tended to become a kind of competitive game, as field guides and travel opportunities have become ever more available for remote areas, and high-quality binoculars or high-resolution spotting scopes are being increasingly carried by affluent birders. Among "birders," learning about a particular species or a single bird group isn't the primary goal; instead the main object is to tally as many species as can be identified (seen or heard) in the shortest possible time. I have always tended to dismiss this approach as merely a kind of numerical ornithomania, although it is certainly fun to tally up one's daily bird list and mentally compare it with other earlier visits.

With all these attractive features, it has always been hard for me to understand why *everybody* doesn't become caught up by the appeal of birds, although if innate ornithophilia were a universal human trait it would tend to result in wholly clogged-up nature preserve trails, and the roads of wildlife refuges would be even more crowded than is now the case. Nevertheless, at the risk of possibly turning a few more people into hard-core bird-watchers, or at least tolerant fellow travelers, I offer this diverse collection of articles, essays, and sketches.

All of the articles appearing here originally were published in national magazines such as *Natural History,* and all of the introductory essays were likewise originally published as editorials in the *Lincoln Journal-Star* newspaper. However, minor text changes and updating of information have been needed in some of the articles and essays. The pen-and-ink drawings are all my own. I must thank Ms. Shannon Davies of the University of Texas Press, who originally suggested assembling a retrospective collection of some of my popular writings for publication, and who helped to get the necessary editorial support required to convert it into an actual book.

EARTH, WATER, AND SKY

I. *Earth*

STRAY FEATHERS
IN THE DUST

*Male Greater
Prairie-Chicken
in display*

Sacred Places and the Voices of Ancestors

NEARLY ALL OF US HAVE SOME SACRED places in our lives, even if they have not been formally sanctified and recognized as such. The most obvious such place might be a family cemetery plot, or possibly an abandoned farmstead, even if the original building that was so important to us may now be missing. One of the important sacred places in my life consists of an unnamed hill overlooking Burchard Lake, in Pawnee County, Nebraska. Nearly every spring since 1961 I have spent at least one morning or evening there, to watch the annual mating displays of the prairie-chickens, which themselves have gathered on that same hilltop for a period probably much longer than the memories of any of the people who have known of the existence of this very special place.

This annual regeneration of the species is attained through ritualized but competitive male displays that help establish relative social status for every participant. Socially dominant males, which acquire and defend centrally located territories, are somehow recognized by the females and are invariably chosen by them for mating. Additionally, a cultural tradition

Earth is evidently passed on to the young and inexperienced birds, who soon learn the location of the display ground from older males.

As I returned to this hilltop site last week, I was reminded that twenty years ago I took my two sons there on one April morning, erected a small tent in the pale predawn light, and quickly set up my own small photographic blind beside their tent. We were ready just in time for the first arrivals, the males that walked or flew into their mating territories to begin their hypnotic calling and somewhat humanlike dancing behavior, which usually continues at least until sunrise and sometimes beyond, depending on the amount of disturbance they encounter.

This year, to increase the chances that the birds would start to display without too much delay, I brought along a tape player and a recording of the males' courtship calls that I made more than two decades previously. As I placed the tape in the player, I noticed that I had made that recording on April 7, 1970, and that it had been recorded on the very same hill overlooking Burchard Lake. As the soft but resonant recorded calls of the males were being broadcast out over the newly greening hills, I suddenly realized that these were calls that had been made by the direct ancestors of the very males that I was trying to attract! Furthermore, these living males would be hearing for the first time the voices of their now-deceased great-great-great-grandparents or thereabouts, assuming that each prairie-chicken generation lasts for only about three or four years on average. In this way, these voices from the distant past would be exhorting their own descendants to gather and participate in the activities they once had so enthusiastically engaged in, but that had now been quieted for eternity.

This powerful realization, that ancestral voices might pass down through subsequent generations and influence them, even though the birds themselves are now dead, made me think of how the same might apply to me. My paternal grandfather was the son of a first-generation Norwegian immigrant, who would impress the value of a penny on me. My maternal grandfather was the son of a Canadian "easterner" who died when I was less than a year old. Yet his voice also spoke to me during my childhood, through my mother's love for English literature and the legacy of natural history books that had been part of his own library but eventually were absorbed into my own reading experience.

A few weeks ago I invited my granddaughter to accompany me and watch, for her very first time, the act of annual renewal that is played out every spring among every generation of prairie-chickens on the beautiful grass-mantled hilltop above Burchard Lake. Thus, I can personally show my granddaughter some of my own sacred places in Nebraska, and introduce her to one of my very special spring rituals. There may be better reasons for viewing an April sunrise while sitting on an obscure hilltop in eastern Nebraska, but I can't think of one.

Dawn
Rendezvous
on the Lek

IN ITS CLASSIC SENSE, "LEK" REFERS TO THE traditional assembly ground or display area on which groups of European Black Grouse (*Lyrurus tetrix*) males congregate in the spring and fall to defend territories and to attract female grouse. In such leks from five to twenty-five males typically gather at dawn, each on his own small plot within the shared lek, to threaten one another with aggressive postures and to call and strut before the females. Unlike typical avian territories, there is no nesting on the lek and little foraging; rather, the area is used almost exclusively for reproductive purposes. The word "lek," in fact, is believed to have derived from the Swedish *leka*, which means "to play," but which also carries sexual connotations.

Of the seventeen other grouse species in the world, four North American species socially display in classic lek fashion. Species of eleven other bird families also perform communally in recognizable, restricted "arenas," including numerous tropical American manakins and various New Guinea birds of paradise. Australian bowerbirds perform similar ceremonies, but in larger arenas where the individuals are more widely separated. Some forest-dwelling grouse, such as the

Sage Grouse
in display

North American Blue Grouse (*Dendragapus obscurus*) and the European Capercaillie (*Tetrao urogallus*), also usually display in "exploded" leks, where the males may be out of sight of each other but within hearing range. Such situations, where individual males are far apart, grade imperceptibly into typical territorial behavior.

Wherever classic lek ceremonies have evolved, they are associated with certain other behavioral traits. In all true lek species, the female performs incubation and rearing duties; lek behavior is therefore limited to those species in which the female alone is able to protect and rear the young. The males are always polygamous or promiscuous in their mating, and a considerable degree of sexual dimorphism (differences between the sexes) exists in structure, plumage, and behavior. This is generally believed to be the result of sexual selection, whereby individuals carrying genes that confirm a reproductive advange for them over others of their sex are preferentially transmitted because of their greater individual reproductive success. Thus the males of lek species are often brightly colored and perform elaborate visual displays. These are frequently associated with vocal or mechanical methods of sound production. Indeed, some of the most remarkable plumages and displays known are found in birds that participate in lek displays.

Species that form leks pose several basic and still partly unsolved biological problems. What ecological situations favor the evolution of lek behavior in polygamous or promiscuous birds? Why do males of lek species often appear to perform in an identical and synchronized manner, when they are clearly sexual rivals? Do females exhibit any "choice" among the males when the grounds are visited for mating purposes, and, if so, are certain males regularly favored by females? Since the males appear to perform the same displays in exactly the same way, can sexual selection account for the evolution of their remarkable plumages and displays? Finally, how are the dangers of predation reduced or avoided by such vocally and visually conspicuous congregations of displaying birds?

As mentioned, four species of North American grouse perform in typical lek fashion: these include the Greater and Lesser Prairie-Chickens (*Tympanuchus cupido* and *T. pallidicinctus*), the Sharp-tailed Grouse (*Pedioecetes phasianellus*), and the Sage Grouse (*Centrocercus urophasianus*). These species differ in appearance from the Eurasian Black Grouse in a few respects. For example, excepting the Sage Grouse, relatively little plumage dimorphism exists in the North American forms. But, unlike the brushlands- and woodland-edge-dwelling Black Grouse, all four species are more open-country birds, and one might expect the males would retain a female-like, concealing coloration pattern that blends well with grasses and low shrubs. On the other hand, males of all four species compensate for their lack of conspicuous plumage by having hidden air sacs in their necks. These are unfeathered areas of skin that expand when the esophagus is inflated with air, thus exposing the colored skin and simultaneously producing distinctive sounds in the different species. The relatively weak sounds are supplemented by louder notes and cackles, and by sounds produced by stamping the feet, rattling the tail feathers, or scraping the wings against the breast feathers.

In all four species the males congregate on their leks primarily in the spring, but they also are active to a lesser degree during the fall and at other times as well. On their respective "booming," "gobbling," "dancing," or "strutting" ground, male Greater and Lesser Prairie-Chickens, Sharp-tails, and Sage Grouse establish and daily defend their territories, which are often only from 5 to 100 square yards in size. The leks are always in relatively open vegetation and in many cases are located on elevations where visibility is unrestricted in all directions. Most display activity occurs near dawn and again at dusk, when the light is barely adequate for vision but when few diurnal predators are active.

Earth The number of males on a particular lek varies among species and with population density. In Greater Prairie-Chickens, from seven to ten males are commonly present, but occasionally there are as many as forty. In Lesser Prairie-Chickens the average number appears to be somewhat higher, but forty males are also apparently about maximum. Sharp-tailed Grouse frequently average seven to ten males, but rarely, if ever, reach thirty. In these three species leks are usually no more than a mile apart in good habitat and may be considerably closer when populations are dense. In the larger Sage Grouse, strutting ground densities of about one per five square miles have been reported in Wyoming, and they are usually well over a mile apart. The number of participating males is greatly variable, from as few as six to several hundred, and perhaps averaging between sixty and eighty. Some Sage Grouse display grounds containing from four hundred to eight hundred males have been reported; such enormous congregations represent multiple leks within which as many as four or five centers of mating activity may occur.

A remarkable feature of these assemblages is the presence of master cocks—dominant males that occupy central positions and often maintain larger than average territories. This situation was first reported for Sage Grouse, but it is also present to varying degrees in prairie-chickens, Sharp-tailed Grouse, and Black Grouse. At the peak of the breeding season, such master cocks are often surrounded by receptive females and are normally responsible for performing the majority of matings on an individual lek. I have observed a Sage Grouse master cock complete seven matings in a pressurized period of thirty-three minutes, while none was even attempted by more than sixty other males on the strutting ground. Each female that had been successfully mated left the strutting ground within a few minutes and only a few females remained after the sun had risen above the horizon. One or more major rivals, or subcocks, are often present, and a larger number of adjacent guard cocks may also participate in a few matings; however, few, if any, matings are performed by the numerous peripheral males.

In the Black Grouse a definite correlation between this social hierarchy and age has been found: dominant males are three years old or older, second-rank males are two years old, and males holding peripheral territories are yearlings. Whether females are attracted to specific master cocks or are only attracted to the center of the lek is still a debatable point. In any case, male displays in grouse are largely aggressive in function, and they are primarily related to establishing and preserving territorial status.

Only a few grouse displays are specifically reserved for females. These include the "nuptial bow," which is typical of both species of prairie-chickens and Sharp-tailed Grouse. In these same species a short, nearly vertical flight, or "flutter jump," also occurs and apparently serves to advertise the male's territory to females. Both the prairie-chickens and the Sharp-tailed Grouse have calls that are uttered only when females are on the lek. In prairie-chickens this call is called the "whoop" and in Sharp-tailed Grouse the corresponding call is called the "pow." Recordings or imitations of these calls will usually stimulate several males to begin flutter jumping.

Even though most grouse displays probably are primarily concerned with territorial establishment and maintenance, and thus are essentially aggressive in context, relatively little actual fighting occurs in these species. Rather, overt fighting is largely replaced by ritualized fighting, which occurs at the edges of territories and occupies much of each male's time and energy while on the lek. In ritualized fighting, incomplete attacks, feints, and prolonged glaring at the opponent greatly reduce actual combat when birds are claiming and defending their territorial boundaries.

Each of the four species exhibits a high degree of species-specificity in male displays and vocalizations, suggesting that the prevention of interbreeding may have been a major factor in the evolution of these display differences. For example, in many respects the plumages and displays of Greater Prairie-Chickens and Sharp-tailed Grouse are direct opposites, suggesting that they could readily serve in keeping their gene pools separated. The Greater Prairie-Chicken has a brown, rounded tail, and yellow air sacs and erectile earlike plumes on the neck. Sharp-tailed Grouse have more grayish, pointed tails and purple air sacs, and lack ear-tufts. Sharp-tailed Grouse "dance" forward in an erratic pattern while rattling their feathers; prairie-chickens stamp their feet while remaining in a stationary position and alternately spread and snap shut their tail feathers. Yet where human activities have brought these two once relatively isolated species into contact, hybridization has repeatedly occurred, indicating that these structural and behavioral differences are not completely effective in maintaining reproductive isolation. This fact—and the general absence of geographic overlap between the species of lek grouse in most areas—suggest that sexual selection or other factors have been of primary importance in the evolution of these patterns. Additionally, the species most thoroughly ecologically isolated from the others, the Sage Grouse, has the most distinctive male plumage and the most remarkable displays of all.

The Sage Grouse is reported to be anatomically distinctive from the other lek grouse, and some ornithologists have suggested that perhaps it is actually a forest grouse that became adapted to a sagebrush habitat and evolved a lek display and plumage pattern similar to but not identical with those of the typical prairie grouse. It is true that there appears to be no flutter jumping, dancing, or bowing displays in Sage Grouse, and the air sac locations and rates of inflation are altogether different. But some of these behavioral divergences may be related to bodily size differences, ecological effects, or other indirect factors. Since it is reasonable that an extreme behavioral and structural sexual dimorphism in Sage Grouse might be expected to have developed through intensive sexual selection, these differences in the Sage Grouse may have little or no significance in assessing evolutionary relationships. However, it does appear that lek behavior in grouse is more likely to evolve in open-country than in forest-dwelling species, which usually are relatively solitary and perform their noisy displays from logs or branches in trees. In leks of the forest-dwelling manakins and certain birds of paradise, the males usually display in the upper levels of the trees in cleared areas near the forest floor, where sunlight penetrates the leafy canopy.

Males of each of the grouse species use the visual signals and sounds produced by air sac inflation as a major species-specific display. In Greater Prairie-Chickens this "booming" is accompanied by a soft, three-part cooing note and an enormous extension of the yellow air sacs. In the Lesser Prairie-Chicken a repeated "gobble" is uttered, and the inflated air sacs are crimson colored. A soft, sometimes repeated "cooing" or "hooting" sound is uttered frequently by Sharp-tailed Grouse, but their purple air sacs are not greatly inflated. Finally, the Sage Grouse rapidly inflates and deflates his frontal, greenish-yellow air sacs several times in succession, producing strange plopping sounds as the bird struts about with his tail strongly cocked and spread. The cooing of Sharp-tailed Grouse is not as important or frequent as a tail-rattling display that is performed in conjunction with dancing. In this unique performance a rapid, lateral shaking of the tail produces a series of clicking sounds at a rate reported to be almost fifty per second, caused by the inner webs of the tail feathers rubbing over the adjacent feather shafts. An equally unusual sound is produced by the Sage Grouse during his strutting, by the repeated rubbing of the folded wings downward and forward over the stiffened, white "cape" feathers of his breast.

Earth The collective noisy activities of the congregated males on leks may have several effects. First, they obviously attract mature females and possibly stimulate their endocrine glands to bring them into final reproductive readiness for ovulation. When such females visit the lek they are given attention by many males but usually congregate about the master cock. Probably a female visits the lek for several mornings prior to, and during the period of, laying, but this point is still unproved. A second probable effect of the displaying males is to attract predators. Presumably a "safety in numbers" concept applies here—at least some of the many males are likely to observe a possible predator, whereas a single displaying bird might not. In Sharp-tailed Grouse there is a remarkable synchronization of dancing on the part of the males, which alternately dance in concert and stop motionless in nearly perfect synchrony. During resting periods the birds appear to be very attentive to extraneous noises or movements. In all species, a flying hawk or other suspicious movement will cause a total cessation of display activity and a possible mass flight away from the lek area.

The advantages of lek display in promiscuous species would thus appear to be several. Obviously, it provides for an efficient perpetuation of the species through allowing reproduction by only the males that are sufficiently strong and virile to maintain their status as master cocks. However, the aggregations of numerous displaying males may perhaps provide greater attraction and hormonal stimulation to females than would lone displaying birds. Although peripheral males are excluded from mating and do not benefit from participating in social display, the "apprentice" period they serve on the outer limits of the lek may better prepare them to hold central territories in later years. Furthermore, the peripheral males perhaps constitute a buffer of expendable individuals that could be lost to predators without reducing the population's reproductive efficiency. It has been recently suggested that lek aggregations also may have a population dispersion effect and might thus fulfill the spacing function of more typical terri- tories, and that leks may function as a density-regulating mechanism through their control of reproductive success in the population.

Whatever the primary and secondary functions of lek behavior, it is pleasant to contemplate that all four species of the American lek grouse can still be observed and studied in various parts of the United States. Sadly, all of the species have greatly suffered from the effects of land-use changes in the last several decades, and it is possible that one or more of them will ultimately go the way of the Heath Hen, the extinct eastern form of the Greater Prairie-Chicken. Preservation of fairly large areas of natural grasslands will probably be the only way to save the midwestern and Gulf Coast (Attwater's) races of the Greater Prairie-Chicken, which today are rapidly declining in numbers and diminishing in breeding ranges. Indeed, the most recent counts of the Attwater's Prairie-Chicken indicated that fewer than fifty birds now survive in the wild. As any person can testify who has known the pleasure of huddling in a blind during the predawn beauty of a clear spring morning, while listening to the ghostlike sounds outside and waiting for the sun to illuminate the shadowy figures, the extinction of any of our lek grouse would be an irreparable loss.

The Elusive Tree Quails of Mexico

Adult Bearded Tree Quail

THE VERNACULAR NAME "QUAIL" USUALLY BRINGS TO mind a group of birds with several characteristics in common. Quails are normally small, stocky birds with rather short tails, and small beaks adapted to picking up seeds, their principal foods. They are essentially terrestrial, and when frightened normally run as fast as their legs allow, or freeze and burst into flight at the last possible moment. Except during the breeding season, they are found in coveys numbering from about a dozen to several hundred birds, depending on the species.

But virtually none of these traits applies to the three species of tree quails or wood-partridges of the genus *Dendrortyx*, all natives of Mexico and Central America. They are all surprisingly large, weighing up to one pound in the case of the largest species, and have relatively long tails that result in an overall body length of from 9 to 16 inches. Their beaks are large and heavy, and are related to their abilities to tear apart and consume fruits, flower buds, and similar materials. Although tree quails do forage on the forest floor, they roost in trees and are often found perched on branches. When flushed by a dog they usually fly up into a nearby tree and peer down, uttering grouselike alarm notes.

Three species of tree quails have been described, all of which occur in moist montane forests, especially the mist-shrouded cloud forests that occur at elevations too high and too cool to support tropical rainforests. These forests, usually lush with bromeliads and epiphytic orchids, are both relatively rare and often inaccessible. Additionally, the birds are exceedingly shy and difficult to see.

So it is not surprising that the tree quails are the least known of all the North American quail species, and many museums have few or no specimens. The species most commonly found in museums is the largest, the Long-tailed Tree Quail (*D. macroura*), which ranges along the western cordillera from Jalisco to Oaxaca, and eastward along the Valley of Mexico to Veracruz. In Veracruz it is replaced by a smaller species, the extremely rare Bearded Tree Quail (*D. barbatus*), which is known from so few specimens that its range is still highly uncertain. Evidently it extends only from extreme southeastern San Luis Potosí to central Veracruz. The third species, the Buffy-crowned Tree Quail (*D. leucophrys*), occurs south of the Isthmus of Tehuantepec in the mountains of southern Chiapas, and also extends into Guatemala, Honduras, Nicaragua, and Costa Rica.

Like many birds of the dense tropical forests, tree quails are far more often heard than seen, and at dawn and particularly at dusk the birds sometimes produce a massed chorus that can be almost deafening. In all three species the typical call is a three- or four-syllable whistle which is loud and penetrating. The native Spanish names *chiviscoyo* for the Bearded Tree Quail, or *guachocho* (in Guatemala) and *chirascua* (in Costa Rica) for the Buffy-crowned Tree Quail, provide a good indication of the cadence characteristics of their calls.

For several years I have been conducting a comparative study of the species of New World quails occurring north of Guatemala, and spent two summers in Mexico studying their ecology, distribution, and behavior. Additionally, I have attempted to obtain live specimens to return to my laboratory, where the birds' behavior can be more conveniently studied and possible data on their breeding biology can be obtained. In Mexico I concentrated on obtaining those species that seemed most feasible to trap effectively and most likely to survive and breed in captivity. Nevertheless, in my request for collecting permits from the Mexican government I optimistically decided to include *Dendrortyx* among the other genera of quail that I thought I might have a reasonable chance of finding. Indeed, I included *Dendrortyx* as a kind of psychological ploy, perhaps similar to that of a bird-watcher deciding to visit Funk Island in hopes of adding the great auk to his or her life list!

This provided a good excuse to travel into several remote areas of cloud forest that I would not otherwise have attempted to reach, particularly in the case of the Bearded Tree Quail, which has been recorded at only a few localities, and has been seen alive by only a handful of ornithologists. Yet since the venerable Pan American Highway passes right through the presumptive range of this species, it seemed a good place to start.

The isolated mountain village of Xilitla, San Luis Potosí, has long been famous for its ornithological attractions, as was described by James Fisher and Roger Tory Peterson in their *Wild America.* Although they did not record the species, Bearded Tree Quails have been collected nearby, and it was thus my first stop in search of the bird. My assistant, Edmund Sallee, spoke Spanish fluently, and we decided that as tree quails are such fine vocalists there was a chance that they might sometimes be kept as pets by natives in the outlying villages.

After being told in Xilitla that the *gallina del monte* was indeed present in the more remote forests and was sometimes captured by bird trappers who sell songbirds in the local market, my spirits rose considerably. From that point on we simply stopped at every village we encountered near suitable forest habitat, asking everyone we could find whether he knew of anybody who was currently keeping such birds. This procedure was inevitably frustrating and time-consuming. Time and time again we would be led over nearly impassable roads to a hut where, if any birds were being kept at all, they were usually of a passerine species, or perhaps one of the more common parrots. Occasionally we seemed close to success — as when we were told by a woman that she had kept a pair of *gallina del monte* until a few weeks ago, when she had sold them, and in another instance, when some birds had been in a hanging cage that had recently fallen and broken, allowing them to escape.

After a series of such frustrations, I was inclined to regard the Bearded Tree Quail as not much more than a mythological creature, and ready to concentrate on more substantive

Then, late one afternoon in central Hidalgo, we stopped the car to inquire directions from two *campesinos* who were walking along the road. Ed spent a few minutes chatting with them, and discovered the incredible fact that a woman in the next village just happened to have five tree quails! I received the news with astonishment, since to my knowledge there were no records of Bearded Tree Quails from Hidalgo, and surely nobody would be keeping as many as five. But we rushed off to the village, Puerto El Rayo, located the house, and there, suspended above the pig trough, were three handmade cages containing five Bearded Tree Quails!

The birds were looking rather shabby, with most of the feathers on their heads worn away by abrasion against the tops of the small cages. The *señora* told us that they had been caught as chicks the previous year, and consisted of two pairs plus an extra female. She also said that one of the females (which were slightly smaller but otherwise identical to the males) had laid a few eggs that had simply fallen through the cage bottom. We asked whether she might part with the birds, but she stated quite firmly that she would not, since her family so enjoyed their morning and evening songs. She said that all five birds sang in concert, which surprised me, since it had previously been believed that only the males sang. As it was getting late, we told her we would return the next day and try to record their song.

After spending the night at Jacala, we drove back early the next morning. But the disturbance when we arrived, caused by the barking of the omnipresent mongrel dogs, effectively eliminated any hopes of recording the birds. However, after considerable persuasion the owner finally agreed to part with them, and we triumphantly left, the owners of more Bearded Tree Quails than I had seen in all the museum collections I had ever visited.

We had been told by the *señora* that their food consisted of soaked corn and black beans. We found that, although corn and beans were certainly eaten, the birds particularly liked fresh fruits such as bananas and grapes, which they tore apart with their beaks. While traveling in the car, the birds "conversed" in low tones, and sometimes uttered low, rattling alarm notes. Not surprisingly, however, they failed to produce their evening or dawn chorus, no doubt because of their new surroundings and the frequent disturbances associated with travel. Wherever we stopped, the birds caused great interest among the Mexicans. They were usually identified as "eagles," no doubt because of their fairly large beaks, and perhaps their "bald" appearance caused by the lack of crown feathers!

In order to study to what extent separation and individual recognition might be important in their chorus activity, I decided to separate the females from the males, and placed them out of sight of each other in adjoining rooms. This accomplished, I set up the tape recorder microphone near the cages containing the males, and left the room. Within about fifteen minutes one of the females began to utter some very faint notes, which were immediately answered by one of the males. This rapidly developed into a loud and alternated call-and-answer series of vocalizations, and the other pair soon joined in, producing a tremendous din. The male's call, sounding like ko-orr-EE-EE, was louder and lower pitched than the female's, and consisted of three or four syllables. The female's answer was more drawn out and the notes more uniform in amplitude, sounding like ko-or-ee-ee-ee-eee. This chorus lasted at least ten minutes, when I had to enter the room to attend to the recorder. In spite of my presence the males continued to pace their cages and call loudly, even though the females had become silent.

A typical dawn chorus did not occur for about two weeks, when we happened to stop at a motel that provided an enclosed garage. To give the tree quails maximum privacy, we put them in the garage with a supply of food and water. At about 5:30 the following morning I was awakened by a chorus of song from the garage, which sounded quite similar to the separation chorus I had produced earlier. This concert lasted nearly twenty minutes, by which time it was fairly light outside. As in the earlier separation chorus, at least some of the females obviously participated in the calling.

Later when I spent a few weeks in Chiapas, we put the birds in a large flight cage in the zoo at Tuxtla Gutiérrez, where they could better exercise and dust-bathe. After a few days of adjustment, they again began to sing from their roosting places in a low tree. It would seem that the function of such daily concerts is not so much a proclamation of territory as the announcement of the location of each individual bird to all of its neighbors. Such evening choral singing possibly serves to allow birds to gather together for communal roosting, since during the daytime they are normally found only in pairs or family-sized groups of about four to six birds. The possible function of the dawn chorus is less obvious, but it is interesting that chachalacas (*Ortalis* spp.), which occupy similar habitats and are somewhat similar in their ecology, perform comparable dusk and dawn singing in concert.

Singing by tree quails is reported to be especially prevalent during the breeding season, suggesting that perhaps unmated males might be particularly prone to announce their locations at that time. Breeding in all three species evidently occurs during the wetter spring and summer months, although few nests have actually been described. Nests of the Long-tailed Tree Quail have been found in mid-April and early July, and chicks of the Bearded Tree Quail have been collected in June. Judging from records of Buffy-crowned Tree Quail chicks collected in Honduras between April and July, a similar wet-season breeding period is probably true for it as well.

The only nests so far located for any wild tree quails are three Long-tailed Tree Quail nests. Dr. Dwaine Warner discovered the first of these in a semi-open conifer forest on a very steep slope and amid a tangle of brush. Dead branches in this tangle jutted out over a 2-foot-high rock face, forming a sloping roof over a cavity some 3 or 4 feet long and 2 feet wide. A mat of dead twigs, branches, and leaves formed a heavy and light-impervious roof above, and a single opening about 6 inches wide led to the nest, which was a shallow depression lined with fine grasses. Two additional nests were found by the late J. S. Rowley in Oaxaca. Unlike the nest found by Dr. Warner, each was poorly concealed and contained four rather than six eggs. Since as many as five to seven young birds have been seen following their presumed mothers, it must be assumed that large clutches do at times occur, although according to natives three or four eggs represent the usual number. The incubation period and the possible participation of the male in incubation and care of the young are still unknown. The eggs of the Bearded Tree Quail are still not represented in museum collections, but those of the other two species are described as buffy, reddish buff, or cream-colored, with reddish-brown spots.

In spite of traveling through several areas which the Long-tailed Tree Quail has been known to inhabit, I was not fortunate enough to observe any birds or even to hear the songs. Dr. Warner has reported that its chorus is relatively rarely heard, and is limited to the breeding period, while J. S. Rowley indicated that most singing occurs in late evening, and although most frequent in the spring, is also heard to some extent throughout the year.

The range of the Buffy-crowned Tree Quail in Mexico has been generally believed to be limited to the Sierra Madre de Chiapas of extreme southern Chiapas near the Guatemalan border. There it is found in the cloud forest zone in association with three other rare birds, the Black Chachalaca (*Penelopina nigra*), the rarely observed Horned Guan (*Oreophasis derbianus*), and the magnificent quetzal (*Pharomachrus mocinno*). Even in preferred habitats the Buffy-crowned Tree Quail is relatively rare; L. Irby Davis estimated that only one pair was present in a 15-acre area of mature pine/oak forest near San Cristóbal de Chiapas. In this beautiful bromeliad-draped forest it occurs in association with the more common but equally interesting Singing Quail (*Dactylortyx thoracicus*), appropriately named for its melodious and complex vocalizations. On several occasions I visited this forest, which is now being badly encroached upon and increasingly ravaged by lumbering activities, but was never able to see or hear the bird.

Conversation with Sr. Miguel Alvarez del Toro, the zoologist in charge of the museum and zoo in Tuxtla Gutiérrez and the foremost authority on the birds of Chiapas, convinced me that the Buffy-crowned Tree Quail also occurs in the interior of Chiapas in the remote mountains between Tuxtla and Villahermosa. Only a single road, which during the wet season is often nearly impassable, crosses these mountains, but it provides some of the most spectacular views of cloud forest still to be found in Mexico. Sr. Alvarez del Toro informed me that he had learned of a live tree quail being brought into a mission school not far from Jitotol, so we again followed the procedure of stopping periodically in this area and inquiring about the bird. Several persons assured us that the *gallina del monte* does occur in the area, and one resident of Tapilula who had captive chachalacas and other gallinaceous birds was obviously quite familiar with the species. He informed us that he had sometimes bought young tree quails from natives who brought them in for him, but found them too difficult to rear to be worth the effort.

In spite of our hopes, we were unable to obtain any more than our original five Bearded Tree Quails. Shipping them out of Mexico to New York for guarantee was a special problem, for not only were the birds considerably larger than our other quails, but also we were quite certain that they would be unable to go without water for more than a few days. After obtaining some special reed baskets that appeared to be ideal shipping crates, we decided that the only way to solve the problem of food and water would be to provide the birds with bunches of grapes wired on the inside of each basket at eye level. This provision was probably crucial to their survival. We later learned that the birds had been held without additional food or water at the Mexico City airport for five days, while the authorities there were checking to make certain that all of our permits were in order. Finally, the birds were released and sent on to New York, none the worse for the long delay. From these birds and the others that were obtained in Mexico we have learned a considerable amount about their behavior and breeding biology.

One of the Bearded Tree Quail pairs nested during the summer of 1971 — the first time that any species of this group has been known to breed in captivity. They excavated a depression in a corner of their cage, and concealed it with pieces of dead palm leaves that were present nearby. The male apparently helped construct the nest, and during the egg-laying period began to call every morning at about 7:00 A.M., uttering a series of hoy-eee notes that were repeated up to forty times. The female laid a total of sixteen eggs, which were removed as soon as they were deposited. These eggs, the first ever to be obtained for this species, were a uniform dirty white. Five of the eggs hatched after incubation periods of twenty-eight to thirty days, or longer than the reported incubation period of any other quail species. A sixth chick was helped from its shell after thirty-two days, but did not survive long. Three of the remaining chicks were successfully reared, and provide additional sources of information on molts and age of maturity. Thus, after many anxious moments and unforgettable experiences, we managed to illuminate some of the facets of the biology and life history of one of the rarest and least-known birds of Mexico.

Quail Music

THE DANGER IMPLIED BY AN OWL'S HOOTING, THE peace suggested by a dove's cooing, and the good cheer represented by a robin's song are all traditional, universal interpretations of bird vocalizations that have nothing whatever to do with the actual biological functions of these utterances. Only by field or laboratory investigations is it possible to gather information about the purpose of bird calls and songs. Some are territorial proclamations or mating invitations; others serve as warnings or threats, help synchronize group movements, increase the probabilities of efficient reproduction, and improve the chances for survival.

Behavioral research has revealed that these vocal communications are highly specialized adaptations that can shed light on evolutionary processes that have affected whole groups of birds. The calls of the quails of the New World are a good example. This group of birds includes some thirty species, about half of which are limited to the tropical forests of Central and northern South America. The other species are North American, ranging as far north as southern Canada. Morphological evidence favors the view that the most generalized, or "primitive," of these species are the tree quails of Mexico's moist mountain forests. The more open-country and

Male Gambel's Quail calling

arid-adapted species, which extend into the United States, are anatomically more specialized, or "advanced," and probably were derived from forest-adapted ancestral stock somewhat like the modern tree quails.

The vocal requirements for all quail species are similar, reflecting basic similarities in their breeding biology. Effective communication between the adults and young is needed to provide maximum efficiency for protecting and rearing the brood. Calls that facilitate the maintenance and regrouping of pairs, families, or coveys are also needed, since the birds depend on social banding as a defense against predators. The effectiveness of alarm, or warning, signals in reducing individual mortality has no doubt been an important factor in the evolution of covey-forming behavior. Calls that achieve a means of individual recognition between members of a pair also facilitate monogamous pair-bonds. Finally, calls serving to announce the location of unmated but sexually active males are also required.

A species with a minimum vocal repertoire is the Scaled Quail (*Callipepla squamata*). This desert and grassland bird extends from Texas and New Mexico southward through the arid Mexican uplands to the Valley of Mexico. It has a bushy, whitish crest, larger and paler in males than in females, which is the basis for its vernacular name "Cottontop Quail." In the winter, the bird lives in coveys of from 15 to 150 birds and ranges over areas of from 50 to about 350 acres.

The Scaled Quail's repertoire consists of an unmated-male announcement call, "whock"; a separation call, "pey-cos," used by individuals of both sexes when isolated from their mates or coveys; an aggressive "head-throw" call, which is primarily uttered by a male when another male approaches his mate too closely; a general alarm note, "chip"; an avian predator alarm call, "oom-oom-oom"; and a distress call, "ciew." There are probably other calls present such as soft contact notes and specialized parental calls.

This adult repertoire develops during the individual's growth. Newly hatched quails typically produce "peeping" notes when they are separated from their parents; this vocalization gradually changes to the adult separation call. Chicks also have loud distress calls, which increase in volume and frequency range as the birds mature. Their softer contact notes probably keep the brood and parents in proximity to each other and persist in adults as calls having comparable functions. The alarm calls gradually appear at various ages after hatching; and the exact time of their initial appearance is probably dependent on specific evoking stimuli.

The Northern Bobwhite (*Colinus virginianus*) is a quail associated with forest-edge and brush habitats. The male bobwhite lacks a crest and, in contrast to the Scaled Quail, the sexes are markedly different in plumage. Their winter coveys average about 10 to 15 birds, and their home ranges are about 10 to 50 acres. The smaller home range of bobwhites is a probable reflection of the greater availability of food, while in the colder parts of their range the smaller covey size reflects the optimum number of birds required to form an efficient heat-conserving ring of birds during nocturnal roosting.

The bobwhite also has a greater diversity of vocalization than the Scaled Quail. In addition to the calls typical of the Scaled Quail, the bobwhite has at least two contact calls, a food-finding call (typically used by females to call the young to a food source), and a female copulation call. Also, two distinctly different calls are associated with male-to-male aggression and indicate differing degrees of social dominance.

The bobwhite's separation notes also exhibit greater variation than the Scaled Quail's, including an increasingly louder series of "hoy," "hoy-poo," "koi-lee," and "hoyee" sounds that serve not only to reunite separated pairs but probably also to space coveys, attract males to unmated females, and repel intruders. Studies by the animal behaviorist Allen Stokes indicate that several additional calls are produced by adults brooding young, including two different alarm notes, a "broody" call, and a "take-cover" call. This surprisingly rich vocal repertoire—twenty-four different calls—is greater than that reported for nearly all bird species.

The acoustic differences between the Scaled Quail and the bobwhite are worthy of note. The basic adult separation notes of the two species ("pey-cos" and "hoy-poo") are somewhat comparable in their cadence, frequency, and harmonic characteristics, but sufficient differences are present to provide for species-uniqueness. Furthermore, the unmated-male calls ("whock" and "bob-white") differ in number of syllables and frequency; and whereas the bobwhite utters a nearly pure whistle, harmonic overtones in the Scaled Quail's "whock" call produce a nasal sound.

Similar comparisons may be made with other quail species. Calls of unmated males typically exhibit marked uniformity within their species but show little variation among individuals, while separation calls generally exhibit sufficient individual diversity and harmonic complexity to facilitate individual recognition by mates. Distress and alarm calls are often nearly identical even among rather distantly related species. Although the typical quail distress call is loud and piercing, with a broad frequency range and resultant ease of localization, the alarm call is a series of soft "pit" or "ick" notes that carry only a short distance and are of brief duration. Distress calls tend to attract other quails and may result in attempted assistance (males may threaten or peck at a predator attacking another quail); alarm calls cause general retreat and stimulate others to utter the same notes.

If the bobwhite evolved a more diversified and complex vocal repertoire in conjunction with its close ecological ties to heavy-brush and forest-edge habitat—and the associated reduced usefulness of visual signals—it stands to reason that forest-dwelling quails should have the most complex vocal signals of all the New World quails. Current evidence tends to favor this view. Compared with open-country species, forest-adapted quails are generally large and rather inconspicuously patterned, with heavy bills and stout feet. They consume insects, berries, seeds, and other materials uncovered by scratching in the forest litter or under the soil surface. They move about in small groups (probably made up of individual families), lack elaborate crests or strong sexual differences in appearance, and are far more often heard than seen by humans.

Some of the earliest observations on the vocal behavior of these forest-dwelling quail species were made by mammalogist H. E. Anthony on the appropriately named Singing Quail (*Dactylortyx thoracicus*). Observing two adult birds kept in separate cages on different sides of a house, he learned that the birds would not sing when they were in view of each other, but did sing each morning if they could not see one another. One bird would utter a series of invitational notes, which was immediately followed by a much more complex melodious series of notes by the other. The duetting continued for some time, with the birds finally stopping in unison.

Until recently, there was no suggestion that the tree quails, anatomically the most generalized of the living species of quails, produced comparably complex duets, although it was known that these species commonly uttered dawn and dusk choruses. Previous observers universally have attributed such choruses only to males, a view that has seemed improbable to some on the basis of the known duetting by related species. Thus, in my observations of Bearded Tree Quails (see earlier article), which included two pairs and an extra female, I learned that the birds sang their dawn choruses in unison for fifteen to twenty minutes at about sunrise. Presumably these dawn and dusk singing periods serve to announce the locations of pairs or families to other quails in the area and directly or indirectly may facilitate optimum population distribution. When together, members of the group almost constantly chattered in low, guttural sounds, interspersed with a variety of

Earth soft whistles, rattles, and other vocal signals, which are undoubtedly of great importance in maintaining contact with mates or family members in densely vegetated habitats.

These examples of the vocalizations of representative quail types suggest that the forest-dwelling quails are more complex in this respect than are their open-country relatives. Since zoogeographic and morphological evidence favors the view that the open-country species were derived from forest-dwelling forms rather than vice versa, it seems that the evolutionary pattern in the quail group has been toward decreased complexity and diversity of vocalizations as increasingly arid and more open habitats have been colonized. Acoustical signals used for grouping birds at dawn and dusk have been lost, and the complex duetting behavior has been replaced by more generalized separation calls. In the case of males, the separation calls have also been variously modified to serve as highly specific signals for announcing the locations of unmated birds. While uttering such calls, these males often stand in relatively exposed vantage points, maximally exhibiting their distinctive plumages.

The overall size and complexity of a bird's vocal repertoire, or language, are a result of its ecological needs for effective vocal signals, its anatomical limitations, and its innate or acquired potential for the use of vocal signal systems. By deciphering the calls of quails, we are coming to learn more about the actual patterns of evolutionary divergence and specialization that these birds have followed.

On Display

THE PHEASANTS

*Male Gray Peacock-Pheasant
in frontal display*

Earth FEW IF ANY GROUPS OF BIRDS HAVE CAPTURED THE attention of humans quite so much as have the pheasants and their relatives. From China to India and the Mediterranean, peafowl have been revered in art and literature and, together with rare spices and jewels, were brought back by early traders to India and the Orient. Red Junglefowl (*Gallus gallus*) were perhaps the first type of poultry to be domesticated, with evidence for their domestication being found as early as about 2500 B.C., in the Indus Valley. By about 1500 B.C. they had reached Egypt, Phoenicia, and Crete, and they arrived in northern Europe well prior to the Roman Conquest. In China, the domesticated form of the Red Junglefowl also was established by about 1500 B.C., and by the time of Marco Polo's visit the feathers of such pheasants as the Reeve's Pheasant (*Syrmaticus reevesii*) were already in use as ceremonial and religious ornaments. Furthermore, the earliest visual representations of the fabulous and mystical Chinese phoenix (Fenhuang) rather closely resemble the Crested Argus (*Rheinardia ocellata*) specimens, which in ancient times were sometimes evidently used as royal gifts from the emperors of Annam to those of China.

In North America we are inclined to think of the pheasants only in terms of the Ring-necked Pheasant (*Phasianus colchicus*) and its near relatives, but in fact there are nearly fifty species that are normally included in this group. Pheasants comprise a significant portion of the family Phasianidae, a group that also includes the quails, partridges, and francolins. These latter birds tend to be smaller and more gregarious than pheasants, and especially differ from pheasants by establishing uniformly monogamous pair-bonds and exhibiting only slight sexual differences in plumage and voice. Interestingly, the major differences between the pheasants and the Old World partridges are associated with the usually monogamous mating systems of pheasants, and their evolution of such associated male traits as ornamental plumages, bare facial skin, and tarsal spurs. All of these are used as female attraction devices or, in the case of the spurs, for establishing social dominance patterns among the adult males.

Indeed, some of the more "primitive" of the pheasants, such as the Himalayan Blood Pheasants, differ only a little externally from their close relatives among the Old World partridges, and experts still differ as to just what criteria should be used for separating the pheasants from the partridge group. In fact, it is possible that pheasants evolved from more than one group of ancestral partridges, as ecological changes made possible changes in pair bonding: in particular, as the more tropical, forest-dwelling, and largely insect- or berry-eating partridges began to move into forest edges and grassland areas, where greater foraging opportunities for seeds existed. The evolution of larger average body sizes and greater accessibility of foods during the breeding season probably permitted males, initially, to acquire more than one female, leading first to harem formations, and later facilitating the total breakdown of pair bonds as females became able to incubate and rear their broods without male assistance. It was this emancipation from male involvement in chick care that set the stage for the development of the remarkable male plumages and displays that are likewise the hallmark of such promiscuous bird groups as the hummingbirds and birds of paradise. However, a few pheasants, such as the Eared Pheasants, have retained monogamous pair-bonding.

In several and perhaps all of the five probably semimonogamous *Tragopan* species, the male is similarly able to transform himself from a somewhat inconspicuous dullard to something resembling an alien creature. A male of these species erects bright blue horns behind his eyes, flashes open his throat gorget to expose a virtual oriental tapestry of brilliant colors, and rises up on tiptoe before the onlooking female, like some unworldly apparition. This display is usually begun from behind a rock or log, making the male's sudden appearance even more spectacular.

Nonmonogamous pheasants are among those groups of birds for which sexual selection has showered on the males a fantastic array of wonderful skin and feather colors, plumage patterns, and elaborate display posturing. The females of nearly all these species are inconspicuous and apparently shy. It is the job of the female to recognize the male displays of the "right" species whenever there might be any danger of mating error. The female must also somehow assess the relative fitness of individual competing males, perhaps on the basis of their intensity of display or by minor differences in such things as tail length or plumage brilliance. By consistently choosing the brightest or most active male to fertilize their eggs, females have presumably provided the driving force for evolution to shape the plumages and displays of male pheasants into an almost incredible range of mating signals that have become incorporated into their feathers and postures.

The average zoo-goer can readily observe the analogous display of the male Common, or Indian, Peafowl (*Pavo cristatus*). The glory and magnificence of this species tend to be obscured by the fact that it is extremely common in captivity and spends so much time engaged in display. However, the male's display and plumage pattern are no less remarkable than are those of the Great Argus. In both species sexual selection has brought about the evolution of approximately two hundred artificial eyes.

In peafowl the eyespots are located on specialized upper feathers covering the tail, rather than the wing or tail feathers themselves. Furthermore, each of these tail coverts bears only a single eyespot, which is an oval design of metallic patterning that is, according to Darwin, "one of the most beautiful objects in the world." Unlike the eyespot of the Great Argus, there is no specific highlight or mimicry of a rounded sphere;

instead the pattern consists of a series of differently colored iridescent rings of increasing size, and these in turn are surrounded by a very pale, almost transparent zone that sets the entire eye apart from the rest of the feather and provides additional visual impact. In the closely related Green Peafowl (*Pavo muticus*), the colors of the feathered eyespots approximate those of the head and eye of the male himself, making the argument for mimicry much stronger.

In the Common and Green Peafowl, the male's frontal display has become a nearly static and statuesque posture, with the bird merely facing the female and occasionally vibrating his iridescent train, causing the patterns to shimmer in the sunlight. What is especially interesting in the peafowl is the absence of any food-presentation (tidbitting) behavior. Apparently the male peacock's plumage is in itself such a powerful stimulus in attracting females that no food-presentation subterfuge is needed to overcome any sexual inhibitions on her part.

To understand the evolution of the train of the peacock and the even more wonderful ball-and-socket ocelli of the Great Argus Pheasant (*Argusianus argus*), we must begin with some lesser-known species of birds, the peacock-pheasants. At least six species of peacock-pheasants (*Polyplectron* spp.) exist, but all of them are limited to jungle and scrub-forest habitats of southern Asia and the Greater Sunda Islands, where they inconspicuously live in the heavily shadowed ground levels of these great forests. As with the Great Argus, their behavior is best studied under conditions of captivity, and one must also examine their plumage at close range to understand its evolutionary significance.

The dullest of all the peacock-pheasants is the drab Bronze-tailed Pheasant (*P. chalcurum*) of Sumatra, which is almost uniformly wood-brown, save for a broad band of iridescent green near the middle of the male's tail. This tail area is only slightly exhibited during sexual display, and on seeing it, one

Earth would never guess that such a plumage feature might have served as the evolutionary precursor to the grand visual display of the peacock. Yet in the closely related Rothschild's Peacock-Pheasant (*P. inopinatum*) of the Malay Peninsula, the iridescent area of the tail has become oval and is bounded by black, reddish-brown, and buffy zones, thus approaching the peacock's patterning. More importantly, these same patterns appear on some of the male's upper tail coverts as well as on his back and upper wing coverts, producing a dazzling visual effect. This species's full display is a lateral display, during which the male stands laterally to the female and tilts his tail toward her while in direct sunlight, simultaneously lowering the nearer wing and raising the farther one to expose the myriad iridescent ocelli for her view.

Very similar displays and ocellus patterning occur in the relatively widespread Gray Peacock-Pheasant (*P. bicalcaratum*). Two points of fact bring the story somewhat further along. First, in this species the male tends to turn in a frontal orientation toward the female whenever the opportunity presents itself. He does this by lowering his breast to the ground while raising and spreading his tail and its coverts in such a way as to form a fan. In this posture, the male typically holds a tidbit of food in his beak and calls to the female. This "tidbitting" behavior tends to attract the female and also places her in the best location for the maximum visual impact of the plumage pattern.

The Malayan (*P. malacense*) and closely related Bornean (*P. schleiemacheri*) Peacock-Pheasants might represent the next step in this apparent evolutionary progression. In these closely related species the male's display is also initially lateral, becoming frontal only when the male is displaying directly in front of the female. Yet in these species the ocelli of the tail and tail coverts are only a part of the collective visual impact. There are also the hundred or more smaller ocelli of the back and upper wing coverts.

Among the most spectacular of all the pheasants are the two species of argus. The better known of these is the Great Argus, which has what is perhaps the most remarkable of all pheasant displays and male plumages. Less well known and probably rarer than the Great Argus is the Crested Argus (*Rheinardia ocellata*), a species that at least originally occurred both along the Vietnam-Laos border in the heavy montane forests and foothills, and in the higher mountains of the Malay Peninsula, where it has been reported from only a few localities.

When Charles Darwin was writing his book on the descent of humans and selection in relation to sex, he became greatly intrigued by the "remarkable case" of the Great Argus Pheasant. The adult male of this species has immensely elongated inner wing feathers, individually ornamented with twenty or more rounded and slightly iridescent ocelli, which are arranged in straight rows along each feather shaft and bounded by a complex pattern of dark brown spots and stripes. These patterns remain hidden from view until the male performs his incredible frontal display, during which he vertically erects his tail and tilts his opened wings forward and upward. This action forms a gigantic oval and funnel-shaped fan that actually hides the rest of his body except for the tips of the two longest tail feathers, which extend above the top of the fan, while the head is turned and situated so that a single eye can usually be seen peering out at the angle formed by one of the wing's wrists. Radiating out in all directions like a starburst from the bird's actual eye are several hundred false eyes.

At any distance these ocelli form a marvelous optical illusion, resembling a series of balls suspended on each feather, each ball lying in a deep socket and individually illuminated. The exactness of each individual ocellus varies somewhat, with those located nearest the feather base more imperfectly developed and rather elliptical in shape, and those located toward each feather tip almost perfectly round. Each ocellus is

Earth shaded below and highlighted above, as would be the case with a real sphere. Since each of these feathers radiates from the body at a slightly different angle, ranging from approximately horizontal in the case of the outermost secondaries to vertical in the case of the innermost ones, it is necessary for the apparent highlighting to differ slightly if the "reflection" is to mimic that of a single overhead light source. Darwin was the first to notice that indeed not only do the feathers that are held vertically have their associated highlights properly placed at the farthest tip of each ocellus, so that they will appear to be illuminated from above, but those held horizontally have their highlights on the upper side, so that they too will appear to be lighted from above, "just as an artist would have painted them," as Darwin wrote.

Great Argus Pheasants are typically widely dispersed throughout the primary forests of Borneo and the Malay Peninsula. Territorial males spend several months of each year announcing their locations by uttering repeated loud calls that may carry about a mile under favorable conditions. Males strongly favor hilly over flat terrain for their territories, and particularly inhabit steep ridges or hillcrests from which their calls can be broadcast out over much greater effective distances than would be the case in a heavily vegetated lowland forest. Both species of argus are notable for the extremely loud voices of the territorial males, which may be heard upwards of a mile away under favorable circumstances. These calls probably serve not only to help space out males but also attract females to male display sites, which are typically located in small openings in the forest or along forest trails where a small amount of open ground is present. With the Great Argus, such display sites for different males average at least 400 meters apart, and in the case of the Crested Argus about 1,100 meters apart, according to studies of G. Davison. A good deal of displaying is done by lone males on their display sites, but the intensity of display evidently increases when a female or another male arrives. The displays of the Great Argus are evidently much more elaborate and spectacular than those of the Crested Argus, in which the buffy-white crest is erected, and the enormously long tail is partially raised and spread. The male then runs past the female while dropping his wings and inclining his body toward her. Males of this species lack the intricately patterned ocelli, or "eyes," on their inner wing feathers, which provide the visual background for the incredible frontal displays of the Great Argus.

The calls of Great Argus males are given on a daily basis, and are especially frequent at dawn and dusk. Calling is also typically done from a specific dancing ground, which consists of a cleared arena or stage in the forest that the male guards and keeps scrupulously clean of leaves and other debris. It is on this stage that he displays when in the presence of a female. Very probably the females are attracted to such dancing grounds by the calling behavior of resident males. Upon seeing a female, the male immediately begins a rather complex sequence of display activities.

The male's climactic frontal postural display is preceded by a variably long period of foot-stamping behavior, during which he marches about his arena in a more or less circular route, stamping his feet in such a loud manner that the sound may carry for thirty yards or more. Such conspicuous behavior may bring the female into actual view, at which point he begins a series of postural displays similar to those of other pheasants. Only when the female has been attracted to within a few feet does he perform the climactic frontal display, holding his posture for as long as possible while the female remains directly in front of him. During this display he rhythmically raises and lowers his tail while generating scraping sounds by rubbing his outer wing feathers over one another and against the ground. Although copulation has not been proven to follow such frontal display immediately, this posturing probably serves as a primary stimulus for the female to become recep-

Earth tive, and may provide a basis for this most important of all female choices.

It is interesting to note that while some of the peacock-pheasants are believed to be monogamous, there can be no doubt that the Great Argus and the typical peafowl are completely promiscuous; the males attempt to mate with any and all females they can manage to attract. Thus, classic sexual selection has seemingly run amok in these species, resulting in the evolution of the longest and most spectacular feathers to be found anywhere in birds. Indeed, recent observations on the Common Peafowl have shown that females are selectively attracted to those males having the longest and most symmetrically patterned trains!

These ornate plumages have saddled their owners with an enormous burden of feathers that must be replaced by molting each year. They have also resulted in reduced flying abilities caused by aerodynamically disadvantageous changes in wing shape, as in the Great Argus, or by the added weight of the long feather train, as in the two peafowl. Yet there are obvious reproductive rewards for those males that manage to survive the three years or more needed to acquire these fabulous feathers. Like consummate sultans, they can then control the reproductive destinies of all the females living within their territories and transmit their own genes to produce possibly still more spectacular descendants.

It should not be concluded from all of this that behavioral and structural evolution is a one-way, highly directional process. Indeed, in the tropical forests of Africa's Congo Basin lives a very remarkable species of pheasant called the Congo Peafowl (*Afropavo congensis*), which was the last species of pheasant to be discovered. Ornithologist J. P. Chapin found the bird in 1937 after a twenty-four-year search. In this species, the male's plumage lacks eyespots altogether, and the tail coverts, although iridescent green, are little if at all longer or different from those of the female. Close examination of the male's upper tail coverts will reveal the faint shadows of an apparent rudimentary ocellus, but it is impossible to judge whether these markings are the relics of some once better-defined ocellus pattern, or if they are but the precursors of a pattern that has not been fully developed. What is especially interesting is that, unlike the promiscuous peafowl of Asia, the Congo Peafowl is apparently strongly monogamous, and thus sexual selection has never had an opportunity to work the same kind of magic that produced the behavior patterns and wonderful plumages found in the peacock-pheasants and peafowl. Like his plumage, the male's display is also relatively simple.

Zoos now offer the best opportunities for seeing these spectacular species, particularly now that a large number of pheasants are becoming threatened or endangered in their wild state. Never again will there be opportunities for such great explorational and observational expeditions as those made by William Beebe and Jean Delacour in the early years of this century. Zoos also offer what may be the last hope of maintaining gene pools of the rarest of the pheasants, lest they be forever abandoned to what William Beebe once called the "slow, certain kismet which, from the ultimate increase and spread of mankind, must result finally in the total extinction of these splendid birds."

Bustards

STALKERS OF
THE DRY PLAINS

ASK THE AVERAGE PERSON TO DEFINE THE TERM "BUSTARD" and you are likely to receive an unpleasant response. Actually, the term "bustard" is simply a combined derivation of two French words, *outarde* and *bistarde,* both of which are in turn derived from the Latin *avis tarda,* meaning "slow bird." Bustards are slow birds as a consequence of their heavy builds and relatively small wings for their body size; indeed, the Great Bustard (*Otis tarda*) of northern Eurasia is often cited as being the heaviest flying bird in the world. If records of bustard weight obtained early in this century are accurate, this may indeed be true; seemingly reliable reports of adult male Great Bustards weighing as much as 53 pounds are present in the ornithological literature. However, weights of these birds recorded in recent decades rarely exceed 33 pounds, and adult males nowadays average only about 26 pounds, or about the weight of the largest swans and pelicans. Perhaps natural selection has favored smaller adult sizes in recent times. More probably, male bustards don't live long enough now to attain their maximum potential adult weights because male bustards, at least of the largest species, gradually get heavier throughout their lives.

*Male Australian Bustard
performing balloon display*

Earth The latter possibility seems a quite likely explanation for the absence of truly large bustards in wild populations. Of the world's twenty-two species of bustards, probably all are declining in numbers, and several, including the Great Bustard, are seriously endangered. Because of their relatively large size and because they make fine eating, bustards have been favored prey by humans since time immemorial, and, in more recent years, they have been the most highly favored quarry of wealthy Arabian falconers. Yet it has been the loss of prairies, steppes, and other arid grassland habitats that has nearly spelled their doom over much of Africa, Eurasia, India, and Australia, where they once were common and widespread. Indeed, as recently as the mid-1700s, the Great Bustards periodically invaded the grainfields of central Europe in such numbers that they virtually covered the fields. These "bustard plagues" were so bad that schools were closed in order that children might help find bustard nests and collect their eggs.

Although hunters were certainly responsible in part for controlling these so-called plagues, the major shifts of land usage from a mixture of native grasslands and open woodlands to an era of intensive cultivation, highly mechanized agriculture, herbicides, pesticides, and all the other earmarks of modern society have increasingly meant the end of historic bustard populations. In one European country after another, the Great Bustard has disappeared during this century, and now these impressive birds are largely limited to the few remaining native steppe areas of central Soviet Asia and China. Similarly, because of losses of native grassland habitats, the almost equally large Great Indian Bustard (*Ardeotis melanoceps*) is now one of India's most endangered bird species. Two of the smaller Indian bustards, the Bengal Florican (*Eupodotis bengalensis*) and the Lesser Florican (*E. indica*), are probably as rare or even rarer.

It seems unlikely that zoos can offer a ready means of saving any of the bustards from extinction; they are so difficult to breed in captivity that only about a half-dozen have been bred under those conditions, and just one with any great regularity. Not only are the adults extremely reluctant to lay eggs in captivity, but the young are extremely difficult to rear as well. In fact Oskar Heinroth, the famous German aviculturist and director of the Berlin Zoo prior to World War II, referred to his Great Bustard chicks (which he obtained by hatching wild-taken eggs) as "coffin nails." Even today no zoos in the world have yet been able to develop any self-propagating bustard flocks, despite intensive efforts on the part of some.

One of the most remarkable and visually attractive features of bustards is their amazing courtship display. In many ways, bustards are counterparts of such grassland- and steppe-adapted grouse species as prairie-chickens and Sage Grouse. Besides having similar ecologies, the males of several bustard species aggregate in traditional areas and display in small groups, somewhat like various grassland grouse display at the leks. Adding to the similarities is the fact that competing males appear to exhibit a dominance hierarchy that is probably based on size, age, and experience. They also similarly utilize inflation of the esophagus, or inflatable air sacs that are connected to the esophagus, as visual signals. These sacs also serve as resonating chambers for the deeply pitched male territorial vocalizations. In the larger bustards, such as the Great Bustard, the displaying birds typically stand rather motionless as they gradually inflate themselves during these balloonlike displays. The Great Bustard progressively changes his appearance from a mostly gray and buff-colored bird to a largely white one, as white feather areas on the neck, undertail coverts, underwing coverts, and elsewhere are progressively exposed. In the early-morning or late-afternoon light, when such displays are typically performed, these displaying birds resemble small bea-

Earth cons of flashing white light that may be visible for a half-mile or so, and their low-pitched calls carry far over the grassy expanses.

The smaller bustards, such as the Bengal Florican, Little Black Bustard, and several others, lack such balloon displays, but many of these, instead, have equally remarkable "rocket flights." In this display, a territorial male suddenly takes flight and, calling all the while, quickly ascends some 30 to 100 feet into the air. At the apex of his flight, he may set his wings and parachute slowly back to earth, while still calling; he may also descend in a dizzy, somersaulting way, with wings and feet flailing the air, almost as if he had suddenly been shot in midflight. Males of many of the small bustards that have such rocket-flight displays have black abdominal coloration, or sharply contrasting black-and-white patterning in their wing feathers. At least one species, the Little Bustard (*Tetrax tetrax*) of Eurasia, also has a pair of sharply tapered and shortened primary feathers that generate a whistling sound during display flights and that supplement his vocalizations. Males of some species have distinctively colored crests, such as the buffy-to-rufous crest of the Rufous-crested Bustard. This crest is depressed and nearly invisible under normal conditions, but can readily be raised so that it resembles a fluffy, pinkish powder puff when the male is in full display. Females of all bustard species are masterfully camouflaged with intricate buff, brown, and blackish patterning on their upperparts. A few female bustards also possess contrasting blackish underparts, at least among those species where males are similarly patterned, a feature that is contrary to the usual condition of paler underparts in birds of sunny areas.

Those who wish to appreciate bustards to the fullest and, perhaps, to see their displays personally must be extremely patient. The birds are usually very shy and are inclined to hide at the slightest provocation. Additionally, their displays are confined to the breeding season and may be performed quite infrequently, often only under ideal conditions. Bustard watching is perhaps akin to waiting to see the Great Pumpkin rise over the pumpkin patch; few people are privileged enough to witness it, but those faithful observers who do so can consider themselves lucky indeed!

Glittering Garments of the Rainbow

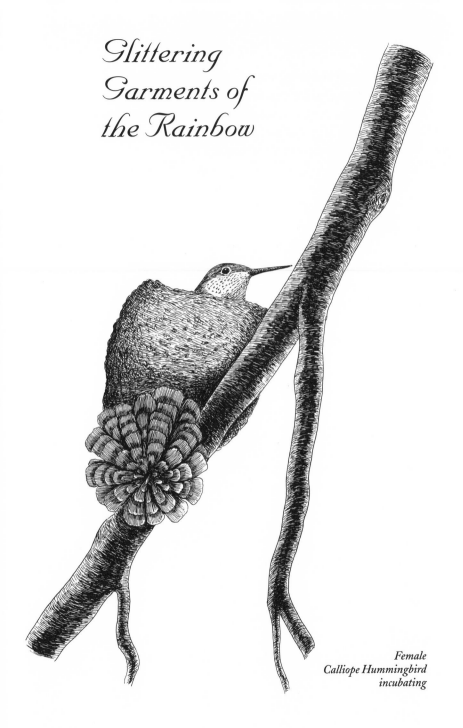

Female
Calliope Hummingbird
incubating

"OF ALL THE NUMEROUS GROUPS INTO WHICH
the birds are divided there is none other so numerous in species, so varied in form, so brilliant in plumages, and so different from all others in their mode of life."

Thus did American ornithologist Robert Ridgway describe
the hummingbirds a century ago, and no writer before or since
has been able to refer to this incredible group of birds without resorting to superlatives. John James Audubon described
a hummingbird as a "glittering garment of the rainbow," and
John Gould called them "wonderful works of creation." The
all-too-human tendency to at first admire such beauty, and
then demand to possess it, has been responsible for an impas-
sioned interest in hummingbirds that has lasted for several
hundred years.

At its heyday in the mid-1800s, the hummingbird market
for collectors and for the ornamental purposes of upper-class
Europeans was so great that hundreds of thousands of birds
were killed in South America to supply Europe. Once a single
consignment, including three thousand skins of one hummingbird species, was shipped from a Brazilian port. And in
one month in 1888, more than twelve thousand hummingbird skins were sold in London at public sale. It was during
this period that ornithologists discovered numerous new species from among the vast number of bird specimens flowing
into England and the Continent. Many of these came from
unspecified parts of northern South America, and a few of
them have never again been found.

Even if hummingbirds were not so beautiful, they would
claim our attention simply because they are remarkably specialized. Probably no other group of birds has as many unique
and rare characteristics as do the hummingbirds.

1. They are among the smallest of the warm-blooded
   vertebrates, and have the greatest relative energy output
   of any warm-blooded animal.

Earth

2. They are the largest nonsongbird family of birds, and the second-largest family of Western Hemisphere birds.

3. They have the most rapid wingbeat of all birds, which can exceed four thousand beats per minute, and are among the fastest fliers of the small birds.

4. They have the largest heart size, relative to body weight, of any warm-blooded animal, and a heartbeat that is the most rapid of all birds (about five hundred beats per minute, which can double with activity).

5. They have the relatively largest breast muscles of all birds and are the only birds for which the wing's upstroke provides as much power as the downstroke.

6. Their plumage is among the densest of all birds, and the feather structure the most specialized, but they have the fewest total feathers.

7. Their relative brain size is among the largest of all birds.

8. They have a unique flight mechanism, capable of prolonged hovering and rapid backward flight.

9. They are the only birds that regularly become torpid at night by reducing their temperature and metabolic rate.

10. Their normal body temperature is among the highest of all birds (approximately 105 to 109 degrees Fahrenheit).

11. Individual hummingbirds often consume more than half their total weight in food per day, and may drink twice their weight in water.

However remarkable these attributes, this list fails to describe their beauty and intrigue. Instead, a list of their common names often provides a better idea of their enchantment. Names such as woodstar, starfrontlet, sapphire, emerald, topaz, ruby, sylph, mountain-gem, sunbeam, firecrown, fairy, and sunangel portray some of the romance with which the group has traditionally been linked. In France they are often referred to as *colibri,* or by the less attractive name *oiseau-mouche,* or fly-birds. In Spanish-speaking countries they are usually called *picaflores,* or flower peckers, while the Portuguese sometimes use the delightful term *beija flor,* or flower-kisser. In the Antilles and Guyana they are sometimes called *murmures* for their murmuring sound, and *bourdons* or *frou-frous* by the Creoles. In various parts of Central and South America their native names include a wide variety of terms of descriptive or metaphorical basis, meaning such things as "rays of the sun," "tresses of the daystar," "murmuring birds," and the like.

The evolutionary history of hummingbirds is necessarily conjectural, since there are no fossil remains to provide us with guidelines. A few fragments of probable swift fossils found in France, from the earliest Oligocene strata laid down more than 30 million years ago, provide us with a rough approximation of the temporal origin of the major group to which hummingbirds belong. It has been generally held that hummingbirds and swifts perhaps evolved from a common ancestral nucleus. This view is held largely on the basis of the similar proportions of their wing bones, their extremely weak legs and feet, suitable for perching or clinging but not walking, and other similarities, such as the fact that both groups lay white elliptical eggs, usually in small clutches, and the young of both groups are hatched nearly naked and blind and are raised in the nest.

In contrast to the hummingbirds, swifts feed on insects they capture while in flight. Some species build tubular nests of feathers and plant fibers on the undersides of palm leaves in a manner similar to that of Hermit Hummingbirds. But the swift nest is secured with sticky saliva rather than spider webbing. And, unlike hummingbirds, both sexes typically assist in nest building and in duties of incubation and brooding.

In spite of the many similarities, some recent authors have expressed doubt as to whether the swifts and hummingbirds are closely related, or whether they have simply undergone convergent evolution toward a similar flight mechanism.

Ornithologist Dr. Jean Cohn has examined this question closely and believes that their major skeletal similarities are somewhat superficial, and no linear measurements exist that have the same relationship to body weight in both groups. The arm and hand bones of hummingbirds are relatively shorter than the corresponding bones in swifts, but the digits are relatively longer. The hummingbirds' trunks are also relatively longer than the swifts', as are the upper arms, but hummingbird wings are relatively shorter.

In most aspects of the wing and its associated skeletal girdle, hummingbirds resemble the perching birds (or songbirds) and their related orders, while the swifts more closely resemble the goatsuckers (nighthawks, whip-poor-wills, and relatives).

Hummingbirds are unique in their ability to reverse their primaries during hovering flight through rotary movements at the shoulder and wrist and in the bones supporting their outer primaries. The larger swifts fly in the same manner as more typical birds, with their wrists reinforced against rotation, according to Cohn's findings. Both groups are similar in forearm musculatures that permit strong fanning action during flight, but for swifts this fanning is apparently associated with speed and maneuverability rather than the development of hovering abilities.

Whether or not hummingbirds are closely related to swifts, it seems apparent that their ancestral home must have been South America, where the largest number of species can still be found, especially the more insectivorous types (the hermit group), which are essentially confined to that region. A bill type of the form presently found in such species as the Tooth-billed Hummingbird would seem to be the generalized hummingbird bill type. This bill combines a moderate degree of

elongation, for probing into the corollas of flowers, with a
limited ability for grasping and extracting insects from them.
From this beginning, progressively more specialized bill types
have emerged as coevolution between plants and particular
species of hummingbirds has gradually refined the relationship of the bill and tongue structure with specific food sources
in nectar-producing plants. In many species of hummingbirds the tip of the tongue is essentially bitubular and probably highly effective in nectar-gathering, while in others it is
more brush-tipped, evidently effective in both obtaining nectar
and entrapping small insects.

It is perhaps the achievement of a very low clutch size that
provided the first step in the shift to a nonmonogamous mating system. This system was probably imposed through selection favoring small body size, thus improving hovering
abilities and survival on limited food resources as the birds
became progressively more nectarivorous. Quite possibly the
earliest hummingbirds, like the swifts, were monogamous,
with both sexes participating in incubation and brooding.
Although some swifts lay clutches of up to six eggs, the re-
duction of the clutch size in hummingbirds to, almost invariably, two eggs has reduced both the energy drain on the female during egg-laying and the amount of foraging required
to feed the developing young during their nestling and
fledgling periods. The gradual emancipation of the male from
nesting duties may have thus set into motion promiscuous
tendencies in both sexes.

It appears to be universally true among hummingbirds that
virtually all of the activities associated with nesting and the
rearing of young are the sole responsibility of females. Perhaps in no other major family of birds does this trend toward
male emancipation from nesting responsibilities and consequent promiscuous mating tendencies seem to have been so
overwhelmingly adopted as in this distinctive group of birds,
the beauty of which Audubon believed must cause one to

Earth "turn his mind with reverence toward the Almighty Creator." Yet were it not for this remarkable mating system and a high degree of associated territorial advertisement behavior, the hummingbird group might well have proven to be no more aesthetically attractive than their drab relatives, the swifts, which have consistently held to a monogamous mating system. In adopting an adventurous and specialized lifestyle, involving a high degree of nectar-dependency, a vast expenditure of energy during flight, and a seemingly devil-may-care mating system, the hummingbirds epitomize a unique kind of high-risk live-for-today, never-mind-tomorrow strategy for survival.

The origins of flower groups specifically adapted to foraging and pollination by hummingbirds must remain speculative, but perhaps they at least in part emerged from flower groups previously pollinated largely by bees and butterflies. Plants adapted for pollination by these insects probably already had some of the important attributes, such as blossoming during daylight hours, having large, showy flower parts, production of considerable quantities of nectar, and perhaps sufficient odor to attract not only bees or butterflies but also tiny insects that were able to exploit the nectar without achieving pollination.

To the extent that hummingbirds attracted to these flowers for their insect fauna may have inadvertently achieved pollination, it became progressively more advantageous for the flowers to gradually shift from insect to hummingbird pollination mechanisms by reducing odor production and perhaps shifting blossom parts away from the blue and violet end of the color spectrum that is visible to most insects. In this way the flowers may have been able to reduce nectar loss to "illegitimate" insect foragers, and perhaps also increase the total diversity of available pollinators, thus reducing inappropriate pollination possibilities.

It may well be imagined that the earliest hummingbird

forms were confined to wooded environments rich in the insect life that would thrive among the dense forest vegetation. However, as the birds became progressively more nectarivorous, it is possible that the hummingbirds began to move into edge environments where flowering shrubs, vines, and herbs grew abundantly in sunny areas, and where the consciousness of individual flowers was increased by large blossom sizes and by bright blossom colors, such as red, that effectively contrasted against the green background. At about this time, the males were becoming more and more prone to promiscuous mating systems, and selective pressures favoring increased male conspicuousness were also coming into play. Thus, increased nectar-feeding was accompanied by increasing sexual selection for male advertisement devices such as brilliant plumages and conspicuous behavior, especially visual displays—like aerial posturing in a well-lit environment.

The hummingbirds' iridescent colors provide a basis for visual displays of unparalleled beauty, so long as sufficient direct sunlight is available to create the brilliant effects that are able to transform the birds from tiny, seemingly drab and insectlike creatures into a dazzling array of spectral colors.

For example, I can well remember photographing a male Calliope Hummingbird that had established a territory in the middle of a moose-browsed willow flat in Wyoming's Grand Teton National Park. The bird would appear to turn gray as the sun disappeared behind a cloud, becoming barely distinguishable from the willow twigs on which he perched. Then in full sunlight he displayed aggressively toward me, ascending some hundred feet into the air, hovering, and directing his ruby-red gorget my way. The sunlight caught the feathers, transforming them into a laserlike beam of ruby light, so bright I could hardly detect the rest of the bird. I suddenly had the impression I was being attacked by a miniature invader from outer space. The impression was reinforced when the bird dove vertically downward toward my head, pulling out and ascending again at the last possible moment before he would have struck my face.

The hummingbirds' remarkable tendency to investigate unusual features of their environment is probably related to their high metabolic rates and constant need for finding new and rich sources of food. Almost anything that is brightly colored is likely to be investigated, from a red tin can on a camp table to a brightly colored cap. I have seen Rufous Hummingbirds closely investigate the red stripes of canvas that support the poles on my tent, and of course red hummingbird feeders will be investigated almost immediately after being installed in areas frequented by hummingbirds. This curiosity can occasionally be disastrous—for example, when a bird becomes caught in the sticky head of a purple thistle and is unable to escape, or is otherwise trapped in unfamiliar situations.

Closely related to the hummingbird's curiosity is its apparently excellent memory, enabling it to locate sources of food perhaps remembered from the previous year. Several studies have shown that hummingbirds have a remarkable capability for associating food sources with both location and color, and there is little doubt that such memories are important components of foraging success. One of the most amazing examples of a hummingbird's memory and capabilities for detailed human recognition was provided by Arthur Fitzpatrick, who placed a hummingbird feeder outside his bedroom window while recuperating from tuberculosis in a California sanitarium. Soon a male Rufous Hummingbird (*Selasphorus rufus*) took possession of the feeder, becoming the subject of Fitzpatrick's close observation for several months. When he was finally able to go outside in a wheelchair, he was immediately greeted by the hummingbird, which careened around his head and hovered in front of his eyes. After nearly a year, when he had returned to his home some eight miles away, the Rufous somehow managed to locate him and took up residence near his house. Later Fitzpatrick took daily walks, usually accom-

panied by the bird. The hummingbird sometimes called his
attention to the presence of other animals that he might have
otherwise overlooked, including a half-hidden rattlesnake, and
eventually rode on the rawhide lace that served as a rifle sling.
After fully recovering from his illness, he left his house for a
month. And only moments after he returned and stepped out
of his car, the hummingbird was again there, zooming about
his head and hovering in front of his eyes.

My own favorite hummingbird was a female Calliope
(*Stellula calliope*) that had built a nest just ten feet away from
a cabin door at the Jackson Hole Biological Station in the
Tetons. Like those of all hummingbirds, the nest had been
constructed largely of spider webbing, lined internally with
willow cotton, and externally "decorated" with flakes of lichens and wood bark, causing it to blend imperceptibly with
the pine branch on which it was placed.

The deception was further enhanced by the nest's similarity to a pine cone, and it was placed among a small cluster of
similarly sized cones. The tiny nest was fully protected from
rain and hail by an overhanging branch directly above. The
nesting tree was situated at the eastern edge of a pine grove,
and the nest so located that the very first rays of the rising
sun would illuminate the nest and begin to warm it and the
brooding bird immediately after sunrise.

Nesting directly above a dirt path leading to the cabin, the
female soon became accustomed to a good deal of human
traffic passing by only a few feet below her, and would toler-
ate prolonged observation by a careful observer from only a
few yards away. One day, while observing the bird, I was visited by the station's director. He stopped by to chat with me,
standing almost immediately under the nest, with his broad-
brimmed cowboy hat nearly touching the branch on which
the nest was situated. The brooding female finally could stand
it no longer, and began buzzing the hat in tight circles, skim-
ming around and just above the brim as if it were a racetrack,

Earth while the director remained blissfully unaware of the infuriated creature whirling madly above! I didn't want to mention the bird to him, since I felt that as few people as possible should know of her whereabouts in order to keep the disturbance level low, but tried to keep a straight face and maintain a polite conversation while watching the hummingbird turning the air blue with high-pitched obscenities, and making mad dashes around the Stetson.

He finally left, completely unaware of the high drama that had transpired only a few inches above his head, and the dauntless female returned to her brooding once again!

Hummingbirds are cherished for just such displays and other behaviors and attributes that seem to mirror a gamut of qualities shared, or aspired to, by their human admirers. Avoiding anthropomorphizing the avian world is good practice, but in the case of these magnificent little creatures, it is nearly impossible.

II. *Water*

A RIVER
OF TIME

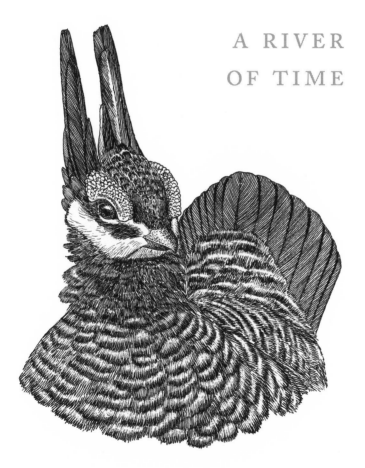

*Long-billed Curlew
calling in flight*

Adrift in Time
on the Niobrara River

LAST WEEKEND I DRIFTED IN A CANOE THROUGH NEARLY 15 million years of time. The time warp began with my witnessing of fossil rhinos and three-toed horse bones being excavated at a famous Miocene fossil site near Norden Bridge, on the Niobrara River of northern Nebraska, and ended with some frosty, clear, and astonishingly star-studded nights that brought an abrupt end to the summer of 1995.

The trip was also a personal clock-setting experience for me—I had last canoed the Niobrara about twenty years previously, during a dam construction controversy over this portion of the Niobrara that finally resulted in a well-deserved death for the ecologically disastrous boondoggle. Also gone is Loren Wilson, an old friend who helped to save the river from ecological destruction by the dam, and in whose memory a memorial marker has recently been erected near its north bank. As I looked at the memorial I realized that he had been born after me, and his life had been briefer than mine already is, but that his legacy to preserve the integrity of the river will last indefinitely.

It is much easier to love the Niobrara River than to extol

Water the understated beauties of my favorite Nebraska stream, the Platte. The Niobrara has uncounted shady canyons decorated by trickling brooks and hidden, lacelike waterfalls, has exposed vertical bluffs whose layered horizontal bands of sand and clay have written the earth's recent geological history as clearly and logically as the chapters of a book, and has just enough in the way of rapid water to prevent one from falling asleep at the paddle. What is most audible when one is paddling the river is the sound of water lapping at the canoe, of wind rustling the leaves of shoreline cottonwood trees, of an occasional Long-billed Curlew screaming its annoyance over our intrusion into its breeding territory, and the constant liquid sounds of softly running water. What is absent are ringing telephones, traffic noises, sports broadcasters excitedly blaring out inane comments on, and endless details about, the Cornhuskers' most recent touchdown over yet another obscure, mismatched opponent, and all the other noise pollution that we increasingly take for granted as a partial price of modern living.

What is especially unforgettable about canoeing the Niobrara are the vignettes one acquires of the people who live along the river and scratch honest livings from it—the sight of a ranch wife balancing twin daughters on her hips as she simultaneously cooks dinner, her husband expertly handling a team of workhorses and equipment, and an array of mostly mongrel ranch dogs that invariably seem to be delighted whenever they are only minimally recognized as being part of the overall scene.

The lives of rivers are much like human lives. They rush madly about, dashing wildly here and there during their youths, gradually becoming more predictable and reliable as they mature, grading into serenity and contemplative majesty in their old age, finally drifting into obscurity and death by merging with some larger river or the sea. The Niobrara is a river that Nebraskans should recognize as not only being as much a historical heritage as our most famous native son and most authentic hero, Crazy Horse, but also as a potential source of geological and biological instruction and of endless recreational pleasure. No other river in the state cuts through geological time as does the Niobrara, and no other activity cuts through the complexities and frustrations of modern life as does a canoe slicing through its clear waters like a knife through soft clay.

What is especially worth remembering while thus enjoying the Niobrara is the effort made and price paid by the many people who strove to protect the river from its ecological destruction and, more recently, from its commercial overdevelopment. What is worth forgetting during a trip down the river are such things as the daily oscillations of the stock market, the current price of gasoline or wheat, and the most recent favorite topic of television talk-show hosts. What is most worth carrying away from the Niobrara are one's individual memories of the land, the sky, and the natural landscape, plus the knowledge that the river will also run through the lives and dreams of the next generation just as it does through ours.

The Evolution of Duck Courtship

Male North American Ruddy Duck in display

BECAUSE THE WORD "COURTSHIP" IS SO IMBUED WITH human connotations, it may be debated whether the term should be applied to nonhuman reproductive behavior patterns. Nonetheless, analogous mating responses can be observed in many vertebrates, and it is instructive to ponder the reasons why such activities often bear a more than passing similarity to human courtship.

The similarities can be partially explained by considering reproductive efficiency. Since terrestrial vertebrates no longer reproduce in a watery medium that would permit simple external fertilization, it is vital that behavioral and structural adaptations be present that will allow for the direct transfer of sperm cells from male to female. Additionally, a prolonged association between reproductively active individuals provides maximum opportunities for synchronizing sexual cycles and preventing mismatings between species. Finally, most of these advanced vertebrates produce relatively few offspring, and it is therefore advantageous if a maximum amount of parental care is available to favor their survival. For such reasons, responses favoring the establishment of individual sexual associations, or "pair bonds," have evolved in some vertebrate groups.

In mammals, monogamous pair-bonds are relatively rare and are well developed only among certain groups that give birth to highly dependent, or altricial, offspring. Monogamy among mammals is especially typical of those species, such as various carnivores, in which both the female and young must rely on the male for food gathering. However, the majority of birds produce altricial young and typically form monogamous pairs that normally persist through a single breeding season. Avian polygamy or promiscuity is primarily limited to those species producing precocial young that are easily able to forage for themselves shortly after hatching, to various species that nest near relatively unlimited food supplies so that the female alone can provide for the young, and to socially parasitic species that do not have to rear their own offspring.

It could therefore be expected that ducks, having precocial young, might tend to be polygamous, if not promiscuous. This appears to be the case for only a very few species, such as the Australian Musk Duck (*Biziura lobata*). However, the great majority of ducks annually form relatively clear-cut pair bonds which usually break up when the female begins her incubation. In only a few duck species does the male remain with the female and help care for the young, and these are mostly tropical species with prolonged or irregular breeding seasons. The biologist is thus inclined to try to account for the possible value of such prenesting pair-bonds in ducks, and to determine the functions of the elaborate courtship ceremonies performed during the period of pair formation.

The courtship of ducks is remarkable in several aspects. In temperate zones it generally begins very early, usually on the wintering grounds, so courtship is not a manifestation of territorial proclamation and defense as is the case with many songbirds. Nor, because of its early initiation, is courtship closely correlated with gonad growth and fertilization; rather, pair formation is normally completed prior to the period of maximum gonadal activity. Therefore, reproductive behavior in ducks may be conveniently divided into an early phase of conspicuous displays associated with actual pair formation, followed by the later phase, with less elaborate behavior patterns concerned with pair bond maintenance and fertilization. Two possible advantages of the considerable time lag between pair formation and egg-laying are that it decreases the likelihood of uncorrected mismatings between species and, furthermore, provides the female with the protection of a mate to ward off unmated males that might attempt to rape her.

The relatively stereotyped postures and calls, or "displays," associated with pair formation presumably originated as a re-

Social courtship by American Wigeon (A),
Yellow-billed Teal (B), Falcated Duck (C), and Mallard (D)

sult of various evolutionary factors. For example, the adult sex ratio of ducks is characterized by an excess of males, probably as a reflection of the greater dangers endured by the females during nesting. As a result, not all males are able to obtain mates, and a spirited competition among them naturally ensues. Therefore, those males having brighter plumages, stronger sexual responses, or increased social dominance will be at an advantage and will tend to be more successful in reproducing. Insofar as these differences have genetic origins one might expect a gradual evolution of more elaborate male plumages and displays. Thus, male ducks have generally more complex displays and brighter plumages than do females, which must remain inconspicuously colored if they are to nest successfully in the presence of predators. If such sexual selection were the only factor affecting male plumages and displays, one might well imagine that different species could be very similar in these respects, just as females are relatively similar in their plumages and vocalizations. But this is not the case, and it is a fact that no two species of ducks that are native to the same region have identical plumages or pair-forming displays.

Such diversity would suggest that a major influence in the evolution of male courtship behavior is the need for achieving "species recognition," or a means of ensuring that females will be readily able to recognize and therefore mate only with males of their own species. It is generally true that males of many animal species are much less discriminating in their species-specific attraction to females than are females to males. The maintenance of such species' genetic integrity depends largely upon the females' ability to perceive the "proper" combination of male traits. It is presumably for this reason that such a variety of male plumages and elaborate courtship displays has evolved among birds. On the other hand, displays associated with pair maintenance and fertilization occur only after species recognition has been achieved. Such displays understandably show much less diversity within large groups of waterfowl.

We may therefore predict that distinctive pair-forming displays and male plumages will be present in groups of ducks having a considerable number of closely related species occupying roughly the same geographic area. In North America this criterion is fully met by the typical dabbling ducks (primarily *Anas* spp.). Thus, such abundant and wide-ranging ducks as the Mallard (*A. platyrhynchos*), Pintail (*A. acuta*), Gadwall (*A. strepera*), Green-winged Teal (*A. crecca*), Blue-winged Teal (*A. discors*), Cinnamon Teal (*A. cyanoptera*), American Wigeon (*A. americana*), and Northern Shoveler (*Spatula clypeata*) all have unique display repertoires and brighter male nuptial plumages that readily distinguish sexes. The remaining dabblers, in which males are inconspicuous and closely resemble females, include the American Black Duck (*A. rubripes*), Mottled Duck (*A. fulvigula*), and Mexican Duck (*A. p. diazi*). All of these are mallardlike birds, which prior to historical times bred in areas where few, if any, mallards or other dabblers occurred. We might, in fact, regard them as mallards "in disguise," for not only are the males' displays and calls indistinguishable from those of mallards, but also the females' plumages and vocalization are mallardlike. Indeed, recent changes in the mallard's distribution have resulted in hybridization between mallards and these populations in every region where they have come into contact.

The courtship displays typical of mallards may be used as examples of the male pair-forming displays of most dabbling ducks. Not one, but several different postures and calls are present, all apparently having evolved from simpler, nondisplay responses including body-maintenance, or "comfort," activities, such as preening or shaking. Three courtship displays are especially frequent and conspicuous among mallards, and all involve variously stretching the neck and uttering a single or multiple whistle. These displays were first accurately described by the famous German biologist Konrad Lorenz, who gave them descriptive names that have been translated as "grunt-whistle," "down-up," and "head-up-tail-up." It is fairly clear that the grunt-whistle represents a stereotyped, or "ritualized," modification of normal body shaking, and that the down-up is a similarly exaggerated form of drinking; but the head-up-tail-up is of less obvious origin.

This last display is actually only part of a complex sequence of postures, beginning when the male suddenly whistles while stretching his neck vertically, at the same time raising the tail and lifting his folded wings, thus exposing the purple wing-speculum pattern. This head-up-tail-up phase is usually performed at profile view to a specific female, and so provides maximum visual impact. The male then turns his head to point the bill toward the courted bird, and usually holds this rigid posture for a short time as he reorients his entire body toward the female. The male then typically lowers his head almost to the water and swims rapidly past her in a manner called "nod swimming," and finally terminates the sequence by raising his head and simultaneously directing his blackish nape feathers toward the female. Several other postures and calls also occur, but they appear to be less significant in the mallard's pair-forming activities.

Although the grunt-whistle, down-up, and head-up-tail-up also occur singly or in combination in several of the North American dabbling ducks, only the mallardlike ducks possess exactly this same repertoire of postures and calls. Thus, the male Green-winged Teal performs the same three displays much more rapidly, with different relative display frequencies and vocalizations, and additionally has a "bridling" display, which involves drawing the head backward, that is lacking in mallard courtship. The male Gadwall lacks both bridling and nod swimming, and furthermore, his head-up-tail-up display is sequentially "linked" to the immediately ensuing down-up posture. The pintail, however, lacks the down-up display, and in this species there is a significant, although delayed, linkage between the grunt-whistle and the head-up-tail-up, which usually occur about one second apart. The pintail also seemingly lacks a functional nod-swimming display, although it is present in an extremely rudimentary form. The American Wigeon, shoveler, Cinnamon Teal, and Blue-winged Teal all completely lack these particular displays, and instead have other species-diagnostic responses.

In a similar fashion, such interspecific diversity distinguishing the basic similarities of male plumages and displays can be seen in other North American waterfowl. All of the typical diving ducks (*Aythya* spp.) exhibit certain male displays such as "head-throws," "sneak" postures, and "kinked-neck" calls, but these displays differ greatly in their visual and acoustical characteristics. Likewise, the three larger species of eiders (*Somateria* spp.) share certain movements and postures associated with cooing sounds, but each species has a diagnostic combination of displays that identifies it as decisively as its male plumage pattern. Several species of ducks having no near relatives in North America also exhibit relatively elaborate male plumages and displays, as does, for example, the Ruddy Duck (*Oxyura jamaicensis*). In such species it must be presumed that competition among males for mates has by itself been effective in the evolution and maintenance of these displays. Additionally, the male Ruddy Duck utilizes his remarkable breast drumming, or "bubbling," display both as a sexual response toward females and as a territorial advertisement display toward other males.

It is likely that such pair-forming displays are entirely innate, as suggested by their stereotyped performance among all the individual males of a species. Furthermore, hand-reared male ducks that have never been exposed to experienced males will, when placed in an appropriate situation, perform their displays without a single mistake from the first time they are attempted. Likewise, newly hatched male ducklings have been

Social courtship by Surf Scoter (A), Common Eider (B),
Common Goldeneye (C), and Hooded Merganser (D)

stimulated to perform species-typical courtship displays by male hormone treatments. Finally, it has been recently reported that when mallards are reared with a foster mother of another species or with foster broodmates of a different species they do not exhibit that species' displays upon maturing. However, males reared under such conditions will usually become sexually imprinted on their foster species and may later mate with such females in preference to their own kind. Similarly reared female mallards, on the other hand, have a strong innate species-recognition mechanism that enables them to mate correctly in a later choice situation.

An additional proof of the hereditary basis for these species-typical displays lies in the intermediate responses performed by hybrid individuals. The relative fertility among hybrid ducks is usually great, and it is therefore often possible to hybridize species having widely differing male plumages and displays. For example, mallards and Northern Pintails have been repeatedly hybridized in captivity, and a few wild hybrids of this type are shot by hunters almost every year. Their frequency in the wild is small, but their very occurrence poses two important problems: Are they reproductively active enough to compete with parental types for mates and, if so, what sorts of display repertoires do they possess?

First-generation hybrids between mallards and Northern Pintails have plumages and bodily proportions almost exactly intermediate between the parental types, as if the parents' genes were neatly blended in an equal mixture. Of greater interest is that their male display repertoires are also a composite combination of the mallard's and pintail's. Thus, such hybrids evidently lack the down-up display altogether, and their nod swimming is performed in a manner that is intermediate between the parental types. The hybrids are fully fertile, but under wild conditions the males would probably fail to obtain mates because of their intermediate plumages and displays, as well as their apparently reduced competitive responses. In captivity, however, the hybrids may be backcrossed with either parental species or with one another to produce second-generation hybrids. This procedure was first systematically carried out by the great waterfowl authority John C. Phillips, who found that second-generation males exhibit some individual variation indicating separation of mallard and pintail plumage traits had occurred, although less than he observed in crosses that involved only mallardlike species.

I repeated this experiment at the Round Lake Waterfowl Station in Minnesota, to obtain more specific information on the degree of plumage segregation in the second generation, and also to determine whether a similar segregation of behavioral traits related to pair formation could be detected. Twenty-three second-generation males were reared, of which about half were selected for behavioral study. These males varied greatly in their nuptial plumages, with some individuals so closely approaching the mallard type that they could scarcely be distinguished from pure mallards, while other males exhibited pintail-like plumages. Of greater interest was my student Roger Sharpe's finding that the mallardlike males performed their displays in a distinctly mallardlike manner. Some of these individuals were the only ones to perform the down-up display, for example. On the other hand, the most pintail-like males were also pintail-like in their displays, especially with regard to the details of the head-up-tail-up sequence.

Our results support the view that these males' displays are as much a reflection of the species' genetic constitution as are their plumage characteristics, and thus may be used to help characterize or define a species. The degree of individual variation observed in the second-generation males' plumages and displays was surprisingly great, suggesting that perhaps the genetic bases of these traits are relatively simpler than one might have otherwise supposed. Such simplicity of control would help to account for the occasional occurrence of indi-

vidual mallards and pintails that perform their courtship displays in an atypical manner. Thus, males of both species have
been observed performing bridling as courtship display, although in these species bridling normally occurs only as a
postcopulatory response. Interestingly, this same display
anomaly has also been found in some of the hybrid males.

   With simple genetic control of male display patterns thus
indicated, their resultant susceptibility to changing pressures
of natural selection makes the use of male display characteristics less valuable as a criterion of evolutionary relationships
than Konrad Lorenz once enthusiastically proposed. However, other behavioral criteria such as female displays and various displays associated with pair maintenance and fertilization are much more uniform among related species and often
provide valuable evidence concerning evolutionary relationships. Therefore, the fascination of pair-forming displays in
male ducks now lies, not so much in their taxonomic applica-
tions, as in understanding their obviously adaptive functions,
such as maintaining reproductive isolation between closely
related species. Thus, it is a pleasant mental exercise to try to
predict what a particular unstudied species' male courtship
displays might consist of, based on a prior knowledge of the
displays of its nearest relatives, the presence in the same area
of related species whose displays are already known, and the
clues provided by the male plumage of the species itself, since
displays evolve with and frequently expose species-specific
plumage features. The usual result of such contemplations,
upon learning the facts, is the chagrin of discovering that the
results of natural selection often represent a seemingly more
imaginative solution to the question than do the musings of
flesh-and-blood biologists.

*Adult male Musk Duck
chasing a diving beetle*

The Elusive Musk Duck

IF ONE WERE TO TRY TO CHOOSE THE MOST remarkable duck in the world, serious consideration would have to be given the Australian Musk Duck (*Biziura lobata*) of the family Anatidae. Among its unusual features are the great dimorphism of the sexes (males weigh eight pounds or more and are about three feet from bill to tail; females weigh two to three pounds and measure about two feet), the leathery pendant lobe that is located on the lower mandible, the strong odor of musk that is prominent in males during the breeding season, and the remarkably large eggs (averaging one-half pound). To these facts it might also be added that comparatively few people have ever seen Musk Ducks fly, that males have a most unusual whistling call, and that the males' displays are so loud and conspicuous that they can be seen and heard for at least a half-mile under favorable conditions. In spite of all these unusual characteristics, no comprehensive studies on the biology of this species exist. This is the more remarkable considering the abundance of the bird over the southern half of Australia. The Musk Duck is of relative unimportance as a game species, since both sexes are of a dull gray color and, as they rarely fly, make poor targets. Also, the birds have a tendency to inhabit weedy,

Water overgrown marshes and to dive from sight at the first sign of danger. This behavior probably is the reason that relatively little has been written about them.

On reading the available literature on the Musk Duck, the paucity of definite information about it becomes apparent. For example, the origin of the musky odor has not been determined, although presumably it originates in the oil gland above the tail. Second, although the normal clutch of eggs is believed to number only two or three, some clutches of up to five or six have been reported, perhaps the result of several females' activities. Some writers suggest that the large males are essentially flightless, yet adult birds will suddenly appear on a lake in considerable numbers and disappear just as rapidly. Likewise, large numbers will arrive at coastal areas during the winter, foraging in the shallows on invertebrate life. No definite function can be readily attributed to the lobe, which is largest in old males and rudimentary in females, but as it is not hollow, it cannot serve for food storage as does a pelican's pouch.

If the lobe, the sexual dimorphism, and the musky odor are ignored, the remaining features of the species agree well with those of the typical stiff-tailed ducks such as the Ruddy Duck (*Oxyura jamaicensis*) of North America. For example, the tail feathers are elongated and stiffened for diving and maneuvering underwater, the legs are placed so far to the rear that locomotion on land must be very difficult, the nest is built over water, and the eggs are large, white, and chalky. Thus it appears that the Musk Duck is an aberrant member of this specialized group of waterfowl, which includes seven other smaller species. Most of these have elaborate male sexual displays, including the inflation of the neck through the use of special tracheal air sacs or by the inflation of the esophagus. The Musk Duck lacks these structural features, but does have an inflatable pouch connected with the mouth that allows for the enlargement of the throat during display. Although the lobe usually hangs quite loosely and resembles a piece of soft, black leather, it can be made thicker and turgid, presumably through muscular action or the expansion of the throat pouch.

Indications of a remarkable behavior associated with these curious anatomical features have been evident for some time. Australia's pioneer ornithologist John Gould mentioned the strange sounds made by Musk Ducks, including the "plonk call," which he linked to the noise produced by dropping a stone into a deep well. The origin of the sound has baffled many people, some of whom have attributed it to vocal origin, while others have contended that it is caused by the wings, feet, or tail striking the water's surface. More recently, various ornithologists have described a sharp whistle associated with the elaborate kicking displays of the male. The female is thought to have only a few vocalizations, which is unusual among ducks. Partly to try to answer some of the many questions concerning this and several other species of Australian waterfowl, I went to southern Australia. Although the more technical details of these studies have been published elsewhere, the Musk Duck provides such a perfect example of the effects of evolution on behavior and structure that its interest as a biological case study equals the curiosity value associated with any strange and exotic species.

While the Musk Duck has been reported to lack gregarious tendencies, it frequently does occur in flocks during the nonbreeding season. At such times these gather on larger lakes and along the coast, relatively undisturbed by hunters and other predators. The birds are too large to be attacked by fish, and dive from sight when a hawk or an eagle appears. Like the smaller Ruddy Duck and the similar Australian Blue-billed Duck (*Oxyura australis*), with which it sometimes associates, the Musk Duck is a hardy bird. It is edible, and for a period of time there was a commercial attempt to can and market its meat.

As the spring breeding season approaches, Musk Ducks

Water move into places where permanent water areas exist, and which have substantial cover of emergent vegetation such as rushes and cattails. In such areas the males begin to attract the females by a combination of vocal and mechanical sounds and visual posturing.

Unlike the other stiff-tails, or ducks in general, there does not appear to be a true "courtship" that facilitates the formation of a pair bond lasting through the breeding season. Rather, the males indiscriminately display to all females, and probably associate with them only until fertilization is achieved, after which the female lays the eggs and tends them and the young by herself. In this way the male is potentially capable of fertilizing a large number of females; the limit simply depends upon the availability of females and the distance from which they can be attracted. Thus the conspicuous nature of the displays is explained as a result of differential abilities of males to attract females on the basis of their varying appearance and their behavior. (The younger males have smaller pouches and possibly display with less vigor.) In this way the presence of the pendant lobe and inflatable throat pouch, which enhance the visual aspects of display, seems explainable, and the loud splashing and calling provide important auditory stimuli. Yet there is no evidence that the females are sensitive to the musky odor of the males. The surprisingly large size of the mature males may also be related to selection for sexual attraction, but certainly must also be partly a result of their aggressive tendencies. When a male is displaying to one or more females—frequently several will be attracted simultaneously—other males sometimes also approach the group. Should such an "onlooker" male move too close to a female, the displaying bird will suddenly rush toward him across the water surface or, more commonly, dive submarine-fashion and attempt to attack him from below. Usually the intended victim frantically retreats at the first indication of an attack, but occasionally a vicious battle ensues, with bit-ing, wing beating, and scratching all combined amid a frenzied splashing of water. Smaller and weaker males are probably lucky to emerge from such a battle without broken bones, and thus a distinct advantage accrues to the larger and stronger. This, then, could well account for the evolution of the extreme sexual dimorphism that exists today.

In the displays of the male Musk Duck, we can see an interesting hierarchy of forms that appear to represent increasing degrees of modification and exaggeration of normal behavior and reflect probable stages in the evolution of these displays. Not only do the postures become progressively more unlike normal swimming postures, but also the time intervals between them become more constant and predictable.

The simplest of these displays consists of a vigorous backward thrust of the feet that produces a "paddling-kick," in which a sheet of water is thrown upward and backward six feet or more. Clearly this display derives from a stronger than usual paddling movement, thus resulting in both visual and auditory stimuli, but lacks marked posturing or associated calling. Paddling-kicks are repeated at irregular intervals of several seconds.

The second display, or "plonk-kick," is made up of variable tail-cocking, lobe and throat enlargement, and a simultaneous kick by both feet. Unlike the paddling-kick, which is primarily directed backward, the plonk-kick tends to throw water out laterally, and both legs are momentarily lifted from the water as they are pulled backward. As the feet enter the water their outstretched webs strike the surface, thus producing the distinctive plonk sound associated with the display. These kicks are indefinitely repeated at intervals of approximately three seconds, with only slight variation.

As females are attracted by the noise and water movement, the male replaces the "plonk-kick" by the most complex display, the "whistle kick." Extreme tail-cocking, lobe enlargement, and throat inflation are associated with this display,

Water which consists of a relatively weak sideways kick of both feet and a simultaneous, sharp whistle. Between kicks the body is often flexed upward to an extreme degree, as the bill is raised and the tail is bent forward until it touches the back. The interval between successive whistle kicks averages over three seconds and rarely varies by more than a quarter-second.

This species is perhaps unique in that no special preliminary displays are apparently associated with actual mating. Rather, the male quite suddenly mounts and copulates with one of the females he has attracted. This "primitive" method of mating probably simply reflects the fact that pairing in the species is nonexistent and, as a result, there is no need for synchronization of sexual stimulation or a pair-bond maintenance mechanism.

After copulation, the females move into dense growths of rushes or similar emergent plants and construct their nests. Sometimes the nest is built on the branch of a tree that has been partially submerged, as often happens during the flooding of lowlands in rainy years. The incubation period of Musk Ducks is another of the many points of its life history that still remains unknown, but it is probably as long as, or longer than, the three-week period of the smaller stiff-tails. The downy young are extremely precocial, swimming and diving shortly after hatching. Occasionally the young have been reported to ride on the mother's back as she swims about partially submerged. According to one authority, the downies grasp the feathers of the mother's neck, and during times of danger she may even dive with the young clinging to her.

Although few people have observed adult males in flight, I have witnessed flights by females or immature males on several occasions. In each case there was a strong offshore wind, the birds were in rough water near the middle of a lake, and they flew toward the calmer water near shore. Actual flight was not attained until the birds had "run" for about forty yards or more over the water, and even then an altitude of only a few feet above the surface was reached before they "crash-landed" into the water again. In general, it appears that most flights are undertaken at night, and several instances of nocturnal accidents are on record, such as when birds have flown into the sides of buildings.

There are a few cases of Musk Ducks having been kept in captivity for various periods, and one male even survived for twenty-three years at the Wildfowl Trust in England. A female kept in the same pen managed to escape from the male's constant sexual or aggressive attention by being provided with an escape hatch consisting of an opening to an adjoining cage that was too small for the male to pass through. Another male lived for six years at the Berlin Zoo during the early 1900s. This bird terrorized almost all the other waterfowl on his pond by attacking them underwater; his appearance would consistently cause a fast, general retreat to the shore by all other ducks!

The Unlikely Ruddy Duck

Male North American Ruddy Duck
performing bubbling display to a female

I HAVE OFTEN THOUGHT ABOUT ESTABLISHING AN avian "wow index" based on the degree of enthusiasm that is generated when I point out a new waterfowl species to a beginning birder. For example, a male Gadwall (*Anas strepera*), even in full breeding plumage, is unlikely to evoke more than a "that's neat" response, whereas a male Cinnamon Teal (*Anas cyanoptera*) is certain to draw appreciative murmurs all around. Besides the predictable rave reviews that a male Wood Duck (*Aix sponsa*) will draw, there are also two certain and perhaps unexpected prize-winners among male ducks likely to be seen in Nebraska during spring. One of these is the Bufflehead (*Bucephala albeola*), a fairy sprite of a duck that seems to float on the water like an immaculate apparition, only to suddenly dive and later magically reappear some distance away in all his spring glory. The other duck that generates a kind of instinctive attraction and fascination from the moment he is first seen is the male Ruddy Duck.

Viewed objectively, this invariable response to the sight of a Ruddy Duck in breeding condition is perhaps as hard to understand as a teenager's compulsive reverence toward some rock star. The Ruddy Duck has a football player's neck that is at least half again too large for his body, a dumpy body that is both shaped and colored like a partly flattened and rusty tin can, and an array of spiky, often partly missing, broken, or disheveled tail feathers that seem to be haphazardly inserted vertically into his rump. A pair of satanic feathered horns rise periodically from the top of his oversized head, which is mostly white except for a black cap that is pulled down gangsterlike to eye level. The whole scene is topped off by an oversized bill that is an unbelievable cerulean blue, as if some color-blind artist had mistaken blue for gray on his or her palette.

Yet in spite of all these aesthetic blunders, or perhaps because of them, the Ruddy Duck is immediately accepted visually, and is emotionally embraced as if he were some long-lost child suddenly appearing at the doorstep in a clown's costume, asking if he might come home again. In large measure, it is the very uniqueness of the Ruddy Duck that makes him so endearing to everyone who sees him. Although some of his seemingly "unique" features, such as his blue bill and tail-cocking ability, are shared with the Masked Duck and all of the world's other stiff-tailed ducks, he has other, less obvious yet distinct characteristics.

Among North American ducks, the male Ruddy is the only species known to have an inflatable neck air sac. The related Masked Duck (*Oxyura dominica*) is not well studied, but probably inflates his neck by inflating the esophagus. The female Ruddy lays eggs that in proportion to her weight are apparently the largest of any North American duck. The Ruddy Duck also lacks a dull-colored late summer "eclipse" plumage that is characteristic of most North American ducks. The femalelike postbreeding plumage is acquired in late summer, but is carried through the entire winter and well into spring, so that many early Ruddys migrating through the Great Plains in April are in their winter plumage, and their bills are still gray rather than sky blue.

After their arrival on the breeding grounds, the male Ruddys rapidly undergo a prenuptial molt into their characteristic rusty breeding plumage, and their bills seem to be gradually illuminated from below with bluish neon lighting. By then, the males are usually highly territorial, spending many of their daylight hours regularly patrolling the edges of reed beds with tail erect, neck inflated, and "horns" raised, searching for females and possibly male competitors.

In his classic *Ducks, Geese and Swans of North America*, F. H. Kortright stated that the male Ruddy Duck has the "most spectacular of all duck courtship displays." This statement might easily be questioned by anybody who has watched courtship display in, for example, Common Goldeneyes (*Bucephala clangula*), but there is no question that sexual courtship display in Ruddys is a memorable sight. Unlike the half-dozen or so complex and diverse goldeneye displays, the Ruddy persistently does one thing, but does it very well. Inflating the tracheal air sac in his midneck, the male begins a series of progressively faster bill-pumping movements, tapping the underside of the bill on the inflated neck. This not only produces a hollow thumping sound, but also forces air from the breast feathers, causing a ring of bubbles to form around the base of the neck. During this bill-pumping sequence, the tail is progressively cocked forward even more, until by the end of the sequence it is almost touching the nape. After the last bill-tap, the male extends his neck forward, opens his bill slightly, and produces a soft belching sound as air is released from the air sac or esophagus.

This remarkable display is directed not only toward females but also toward other males, and so must serve dual female-attraction and male-repulsion roles. Males also directly threaten and frequently attack other males, occasionally producing spirited fights. Their common response to nearby females, however, is to try to swim directly ahead of them while simultaneously performing tail-cocking and the "bubbling" sequence.

The most common, if not invariable, response of females

Water to all this is a simple aggressive gape and an accompanying squeaking note. They may also even peck aggressively should the male approach too closely. While some suggest that the male makes a wonderful parent, I have never gotten the slightest feeling that the male is interested in either forming a pair bond or even more in looking after any young. He appears interested only in mating, and it is seemingly rare for the female to cooperate even the slightest in this matter. When copulations do occur, they seem to be more forced than mutually agreed-upon acts, with the female submerged for most of the time, and apparently struggling to get away. I have also seen, although rarely, females lying prostrate on the water, apparently inviting a nearby male to copulate with her.

Nests are built in dense reed beds over water that is deep enough for the female to slip away submerged should danger threaten. The water levels must also be stable to prevent a flooding of the nest or a significant lowering of water levels; nests are mostly limited to the larger prairie marshes of the glaciated portions of the Great Plains, from southern interior Canada south through the Dakotas to Nebraska. Drainage of these great "duck factory" marshes has severely affected waterfowl species, as well as grebes and marsh birds. Furthermore, minks, raccoons, and other predators often have serious effects on nesting populations and the production of young.

The eggs laid by female Ruddys are remarkably large, averaging about 75 grams, or approximately 15 percent of her body weight. In spite of this, the eggs are laid at the rate of approximately one per day. The clutch size averages about eight eggs, which collectively would weigh more than the average female. Clutch size in Ruddy Ducks is often influenced by "dump-nesting," the depositing of eggs of more than one female in the same nest. Ruddy Ducks not only dump-nest, but sometimes lay their eggs parasitically in the nests of other species. Little is known of the hatching success of such parasitically laid eggs, although it is probably not very high.

Those eggs that do hatch result in ducklings that resemble miniature versions of their mothers, chubby grayish creatures with darker caps and smudgy streaks through their grayish-white cheeks. The young are hatched with feisty dispositions like their mother's. Within a few days after hatching, the ducklings often begin to stray, sometimes becoming lost or perhaps attached to another Ruddy brood. Probably because they are produced from such large eggs, the young are highly precocial, and evidently require little brooding or parental care following hatching. As a result, counts of older Ruddy broods often fail to provide an accurate idea of actual productivity. There is no good evidence that two broods are ever raised in the same year, at least in the United States. Since Ruddys take flight only rarely, the fledgling period is still uncertain. Fledging probably requires about 52–66 days, a longer duration than in most comparably sized or even smaller ducks. For example, the smaller Bufflehead (*Bucephala albeola*) fledges its young in an appreciably shorter period of about 50–55 days.

With their short and seemingly inadequate wings, long take-offs, and bumblebee-like flights, it seems unlikely that Ruddy Ducks could migrate effectively over long distances. Yet migrate they do, and many move all the way to the Gulf Coast or well into Mexico to spend the winter. Too few Ruddy Ducks have been banded and subsequently recovered to provide any detailed information on individual migration routes or on their mortality rates and life expectancies.

Fortunately, Ruddy Ducks are not highly regarded by hunters. As a result, bird-watchers can take first claim on the Ruddy Duck, and find it a boundless source of pleasure and study.

Torrent Ducks
of the Andes

*Male Colombian
Torrent Duck*

THROUGHOUT THE WORLD THERE IS PROBABLY NO more rigorous environment for waterfowl than that provided by the Andean streams in South America. Rushing down the mountains from an altitude of 18,000 feet or more, tumbling over precipices, the streams eventually merge and grow into such giants as the Orinoco, Amazon, and Río de la Plata on the Atlantic slope, or empty directly into the Pacific on the west side. In the intermediate elevations, mainly between 5,000 and 10,000 feet, a remarkable duck, fittingly called the Torrent Duck (*Merganetta armata*), makes its home among the rapids and cataracts. This bird, which ranges from northwestern Venezuela to the sub-Antarctic climate of Tierra del Fuego, occurs in scattered populations throughout the Andean chain wherever its specialized habitat requirements are met. These requirements include cold, well-aerated water rich in aquatic insect life, large boulders protruding from the stream to provide resting places and foraging areas, and adjacent cliffs with holes or crevices for use in nesting.

Since roads rarely penetrate the Andes in the areas where Torrent Ducks thrive, it is not surprising that few biologists have had the good fortune to observe this species in its natural habitat. In fact, so little has been learned about Torrent Ducks that there is considerable doubt as to the number of species that should be recognized; various authorities having suggested that one, three, five, or even six different species might exist. With such basic questions in doubt, it is not surprising that uncertainty or even complete ignorance has existed as to the details of the Torrent Duck's biology, its feeding, nesting, social, and sexual behavior, and its probable evolutionary relationships to other waterfowl.

In the hope of answering at least some of these questions, I had been eager for many years to study the Torrent Duck. As I had previously studied all of the other forty-two living genera of ducks, geese, and swans, *Merganetta* represented my last major goal.

Water In order to resolve the question of how many species of
Torrent Ducks exist, it was necessary to find as many as possible of the six described forms. This meant stopping in at
least four countries, from Colombia to Chile, with the hope
that the birds could be located at reasonable distances from
cities. With the support of a National Science Foundation
grant, and after a year's planning, I set off with an interpreter-
assistant in July 1965 for Colombia.

I located the northernmost and (in the case of the males)
lightest colored of all the Torrent Duck populations, near
Popayán, where the slopes of the volcano Puracé give rise to
half a dozen streams that converge down toward the Cauca
Valley. I found Torrent Ducks on two of these streams, the
Río Chisbar and the Río Grande, as well as on the Río Cauca
itself. Although extremely wary, the birds could usually be
approached to within 70 yards as they rested on rocks or foraged in the rivers. When foraging, the ducks typically rest on
a large, rounded boulder near the middle of a river; they leap
from the boulder into the white water and disappear from
sight for ten seconds or more; then they suddenly emerge
from near the point where they entered the water and scramble
back up the slippery rock surface. When climbing, they hold
down their long stiffened tail feathers against the rock in much
the same manner as woodpeckers use their tail feathers as
props.

Female Torrent Ducks are a beautiful rusty red below and
dove gray above, and have a conspicuous carmine bill. When
they swim, their reddish underparts are mostly below the water, and only the brilliant bill enables one to see the bird in
the swirling waters. Likewise, the adult male's gray and white
coloration is easily lost to view in the water, particularly if the
bird is swimming so low that only his head is exposed. In all
the male Torrent Ducks the white head is distinctively marked
with black stripes, and the bill is a brilliant red as in the female. These narrow, soft-tipped bills are used in probing

among the rock crevices for larvae of caddisflies and stoneflies, the main source of food for the ducks.

Populations of these birds are never great, and it is rare to see more than a single pair or family at any one place. Unlike most ducks, the male Torrent Duck remains with the female while the young are being reared, and actively protects the brood when danger threatens. There are usually no more than three in a brood, but the young are highly precocial and shortly after hatching are able to navigate rapids and climb wet rock surfaces with astonishing ease. There has been some doubt as to how these hardy youngsters reach the water from the nest site, which may be located high above the river on a vertical cliff face, often in a natural crevice or an old nest hole of the Ringed Kingfisher (*Megaceryle torquata*).

George Moffett had the good fortune of locating two nests of the Chilean Torrent Duck, one among the roots of a *coihue* tree (*Nothofagus*) on a riverbank about 9 feet above water, the other in a cliff crevice some 60 feet above water. After establishing an astonishingly long incubation period of 43 to 44 days, Mr. Moffett observed the young jump from the nest in the cliff crevice and bounce and tumble down the cliff face, finally reaching the water's edge.

I located a family with two recently hatched young on the Río Chisbar, in a narrow canyon bounded above and below by nearly vertical cliffs and waterfalls. After the family was disturbed, the male cautiously worked downstream, stopping every 40 or 50 yards to investigate. The female followed a safe distance behind, with the young dutifully following in the wake of their mother as she negotiated the rapids. Occasionally they completely disappeared as they were engulfed by the spray and foam, only to reappear again several yards downstream. The vitality of these tiny chicks, which weigh little more than an ounce at hatching, is simply amazing.

In northern Peru the Colombian Torrent Duck is replaced by a somewhat darker form, the Peruvian Torrent Duck. It

Water occurs south as far as Lake Junín in the interior, and also on the west slope of the Andes as far as the coastal desert south of Lima, where a few permanent streams reach the Pacific. On one such stream south of Lima, the Río Lurín, I found the Peruvian Torrent Duck in a narrow, steep-walled canyon at an elevation of about 6,000 feet. The river was lined with rushes and low trees, and enormous cacti grew out of the rocky crevices, providing a strange contrast to the streamside vegetation. Here, as in Colombia, I found that the White-capped Dipper (*Cinclus leucocephala*) was a constant associate of Torrent Ducks, often using the same rocks for their foraging activities and presumably living on much the same foods.

In the Cuzcan Andes of southern Peru, in the valley of the Vilcanota and Urubamba Rivers, the male Torrent Ducks reputedly have dark brown or black bodies, although they retain the typical black-and-white head pattern of the other populations. Few specimens of this Turner's Torrent Duck have been collected, and I especially wanted to observe it. Fortunately, the railroad between Cuzco and the Inca ruins of Machu Picchu closely follows the Urubamba River, and this river and its tributaries support a good population of Torrent Ducks. In Huarocondo Canyon, for example, I located two families with downy young and nearly half a dozen additional pairs along a ten-mile stretch of river. Although one of the males of this group had a rather dark body and thus might have been regarded as a Turner's Torrent Duck, the others were not separable from the Peruvian Torrent Duck. So it is clear that the few dark-bodied males found in this region are not typical of it, simply representing extreme variants from the normal condition. This unusual degree of individual color variation among the males accounts for the otherwise baffling situation of a reputedly dark-bodied form existing between two relatively light-bodied populations, the Peruvian and Bolivian Torrent Ducks.

The Bolivian Torrent Duck is primarily found in the *yungas,* deep valleys that drain the moist eastern slopes of the central Andean cordilleras. The Río Zongo, which has its headwaters northeast of La Paz near Mount Potosí, plunges from nearly 16,000 feet to about 6,000 feet in less than 20 miles. A number of hydroelectric dams have been constructed in the river's narrow canyon, but enough water still flows to support Torrent Ducks. As I had also earlier discovered in Peru, the Bolivian Torrent Duck uses a remarkable tactic to escape from danger; it swims over a waterfall several feet high and disappears in the spray below. After this had happened on several occasions, I finally learned that the birds were crawling back into the rocky recesses behind the brink of the fall, and were remaining hidden by the veil of falling water until the danger had passed. One female on the Río Zongo remained hidden in this manner for over half an hour before finally flying out.

South of Bolivia, in the Tucumán area of Argentina, a fifth form of Torrent Duck exists. This bird, the Argentine Torrent Duck, differs little from the previously mentioned forms except that the males are said to exhibit white mantle stripping. However, this population is known to be variable in male plumage coloration, and in general is not significantly distinct from the Bolivian population. Therefore, no attempt was made to locate the Argentine Torrent Duck, and instead I traveled on to Chile to study the southernmost of the populations, the Chilean Torrent Duck.

While all the Torrent Ducks are certainly handsome, none is more striking than the male Chilean Torrent Duck. In this form the facial pattern is rendered distinctive by an extension of black up the neck and throat to merge with the black eye stripe. In addition, the black mantle feathers are broadly edged with white, and the breast and flanks are brown or black.

Torrent Ducks increase in abundance as the rainfall increases in central and southern Chile, and in the lake district between Osorno and Puerto Monte the birds seem to be especially prevalent. Although the ducks also occur south of the

Water lake district in Chile, they are evidently less common, and the nearly constant bad weather of southern Chile makes fieldwork in this region practically impossible during most of the year. In this part of Chile Torrent Ducks are found much nearer to sea level than in central and northern South America, and I located several birds at a height of less than 600 feet on the Río Petrohue near Lake Esmeralda in the southern lake district. In this location I found only males; the females are said to be much less evident than males during the winter season in Chile. Strangely, these birds were much less wary than any of the other Torrent Ducks I observed, and it was possible to study them at relatively close range.

As I had already found in the more northerly forms, males of the Chilean Torrent Duck possess a loud, piercing whistle that can easily be heard above the roar of the river. This serves as a warning call to females, and a similar but softer version is used as an apparent greeting call. The female, however, is evidently much less vocal, and although other observers have described female vocalization, I was never able to hear any. The downy young (as in most, if not all, ducks) also utter a loud whistle whenever they are separated from their parents.

Probably because of an apparently permanent pair-bond in Torrent Ducks, opportunities for observing pair-forming displays in these birds are greatly reduced. Peter Scott once observed some elaborate male displays in the Bolivian Torrent Duck, and A. W. Johnson has observed copulatory behavior in the Chilean form. Both described behavior patterns totally unlike the corresponding displays of typical dabbling ducks, and this suggests that the Torrent Ducks are not closely related to the Salvadori's Duck and the other dabbling ducks.

I was fortunate enough to watch display in both the Colombian and Chilean Torrent Ducks. My observations differed from those of Scott and Johnson, and apparently represented neither pair-forming nor copulatory displays, but rather appeared to be of behavior related to pair maintenance. The

male's display consisted of a strong thrusting forward and
downward of the head, and a simultaneous raising of the hind-
quarters and cocking of the long tail, resulting in a seesaw
movement for which the legs served as a fulcrum. Since my
observations, George Moffett has observed and photographed
this display as performed by Chilean Torrent Ducks in Argentina, noting that it can be directed either toward the mate
or other males, and in the latter case seems associated with
territorial behavior.

In spite of the marked differences in male plumage patterns from Colombia to Chile, these are probably of little taxonomic significance, since much individual variation is known
to occur in some areas. It is quite possible that the generally
small populations, and consequent inbreeding within these
isolated and sedentary populations, account for much of the
plumage variation. Furthermore, the male displays that I observed in both Colombian and Chilean populations were identical and agreed with earlier published observations on the
Peruvian Torrent Duck, supporting the hypothesis that only
a single species of Torrent Duck should be recognized. Similarities in the displays and hole-nesting behavior of Torrent
Ducks and perching ducks might be regarded as evidence
favoring evolutionary affinities with this latter group of
waterfowl.

Regardless of the taxonomic allocation of Torrent Ducks,
nothing can detract from the amazing capabilities of this bird
for living in one of the most unlikely and scenically beautiful
waterfowl habitats imaginable. By adapting to such remote
habitats the ducks have placed themselves beyond the reach
of most human activities, and thereby may be able to survive
better than most Latin American waterfowl.

Common Murre landing

Seabirds
of the Pribilofs

SAINT PAUL AND SAINT GEORGE, THE TWO MAJOR islands of the Pribilofs, emerge out of the Bering Sea like gigantic whales some 350 miles north of the Aleutian chain, between continental North America and Siberia.

These small, remote islands are ideal places to observe arctic birds in late spring and summer. Their isolation draws an abundance of Asian and North American migrant land birds to their shores, which support some two dozen breeding species of coastal shoreline and tundra birds. Approximately two hundred species of birds have been reported on these tiny islands, about as many as have been observed on the enormously larger landmass of Greenland.

The islands also attract some 1.5 million Fur Seals, most of the world's population of that species. The seals, together with nearly 3 million seabirds, other species of sea mammals, and humans, harvest the bountiful populations of fish and invertebrates found in these rich arctic waters.

The rocky shorelines that serve as breeding sites for the Fur Seals are adjacent to those used by at least eleven species of colonial seabirds—one of the most diverse communities of breeding seabirds found anywhere in North America.

Inland from these shoreline areas, the land is mantled with

Water-covered sand dunes, rolling hills, old volcanic cones, and rocky outcrops, where terrestrially adapted arctic species such as Snow Buntings (*Plectrophenax nivalis*), Lapland Longspurs (*Calcarius lapponicus*), and Gray-crowned Rosy Finches (*Leucosticte arctoa*) all find suitable nesting habitats. Scattered marshy areas and shallow lakes offer foraging and nesting sites for Oldsquaws (*Clangula hyemalis*), Northern Pintails (*Anas acuta*), Red-necked Phalaropes (*Phalaropus lobatus*), and an unusual endemic race of the Rock Sandpiper (*Calidris ptilocnemis*), sometimes called the "Pribilof Sandpiper." This bird and a local race of the Winter Wren (*Troglodytes troglodytes*) are the only strictly endemic species found on the islands, although the Red-legged Kittiwake (*Rissa brevirostris*) is restricted to the Pribilofs, the Russian-owned Commander Islands, and a few of the Aleutian Islands.

One reason for the abundance of nesting birds is the scarcity of terrestrial predators. Because of the seal rookeries and dangers of disease transmission, dogs are not allowed on the islands, and the cat population is very small. The few avian predators include Snowy (*Nyctea scandiaca*) and Short-eared Owls (*Asio flammeus*). Only the Arctic Fox, which numbers 500–600 on Saint Paul and 2,000–2,500 on Saint George, is a significant mammalian predator for nesting birds.

The actual size of the breeding seabird population is somewhat uncertain, but surveys by the U.S. Fish and Wildlife Service suggest that Saint George supports at least 2.3 million breeding birds, of which the Thick-billed Murre (*Uria lomvia*) comprises more than 60 percent. Saint Paul has a seabird population of at least 253,000 birds, with the Thick-billed Murre comprising about 40 percent. The other eleven breeding seabirds include six additional species of the auk family—the Parakeet (*Cyclorrhynchus psittacula*), Crested (*Aethia cristatella*), and Least (*Aethia pusilla*) Auklets; the Horned (*Fratercula corniculata*) and Tufted (*F. cirrhata*) Puffins; and the Common Murre (*Uria aalge*). There are also Red-legged and Black-legged (*R. tridactyla*) Kittiwakes, the Red-faced (*Phalacrocorax urile*) and Pelagic (*P. pelagica*) Cormorants, and the tube-nosed Northern Fulmar (*Fulmarus glacialis*).

When I arrived on Saint Paul Island in mid-June to study its seabirds, the daylight period was essentially continuous, and the tundra was changing quickly from a dead brown to a lush green. Snow clung only to the steepest, north-facing slopes of the more rugged hills, and a few tundra flowers were already in bloom. Everywhere, I could hear the territorial flight songs of Lapland Longspurs, which initially confused and reminded me of Western Meadowlarks (*Sturnella neglecta*). The longspurs and less common Snow Buntings have similar territorial flight-song displays—the males circling about in the sky with their tails spread enough to exhibit their white outer markings. Snow Buntings flashed their white wing marks as well during similar display flights.

I also heard the unfamiliar flight song of the Rock Sandpiper, which I had been eager to see and hear ever since first reading that it sounds like the trilling of a tree frog! Indeed it does, and it was strange to hear this bizarre, almost croaking sound emerging from such a beautiful bird as it hovered on fluttering wings above its territory.

Like longspurs and Snow Buntings, the Rock Sandpiper will suddenly rise from the ground, sing while ascending, hover for a time above its territory, then quickly drop back to earth, often holding its wings vertically for a few seconds after alighting, exposing the silvery underwings, which it will direct toward other resident sandpipers.

I very much wanted to find a Rock Sandpiper nest, and one day I was finally rewarded. As I was traveling along a sandy road, a Rock Sandpiper sprang from the tundra only a few feet from the edge. I shouted to the driver to stop. Getting out, I asked him to continue on, and quietly sat down in the low vegetation.

Water Within a few minutes the bird cautiously returned to its well-hidden nest and quickly settled down over its clutch of four spotted eggs. When incubating, this bird holds it back so low that it is nearly level with the top of the mossy tundra foliage; only its head protrudes. The bird had a beautifully spangled back plumage, a pattern of rusty brown, ashy gray, and black, all blended perfectly with the mosses and lichens, hiding the bird from all but the most discerning eye.

When I finally approached the nest to observe it more closely, the bird, apparently a male, jumped off the nest and scuttled quickly over the tundra like an intoxicated rodent, drooping its wings, spreading its tail, and occasionally stopping and calling in the most piteous manner. I wondered how effective this ruse might be in luring Arctic Foxes away from the nest and hoped that, in spite of the nest's roadside location, the bird might be successful in raising its brood.

While the Rock Sandpiper offers an interesting example of protective coloration and behavior, the seabirds are the primary ornithological attraction of the Pribilofs, offering several examples of the partitioning of habitat by structural and behavioral devices that reduce competition to a minimum.

For example, the two species of kittiwakes are virtually identical in size and general appearance, except for the foot and gape coloration of adults. Even their voices are quite similar. The Red-legged Kittiwake, however, has a distinctly shorter beak than the Black-legged and apparently feeds on different foods, taken at greater distances from shore than is typical of the Black-legged species. Both nest on steep cliffs, using mud to construct their similar nest cups on narrow, rocky ledges. Some cliffs contain nests of both species in close proximity.

Among the auks, there are several interesting examples of closely related species occupying slightly different but overlapping ecological niches. The Common and Thick-billed Murres are nearly identical in size, voice, and appearance, but the Thick-billed has a slightly heavier and distinctly white-stripped bill. It is more northerly in its breeding distribution than the Common Murre, although the two species coexist over rather large areas of the low Arctic without significant interbreeding.

The Common Murre prefers nesting on flat and rather narrow rock platforms and avoids nesting in crevices, whereas the Thick-billed is a good deal more flexible in its nest-site choices. Where both species nest in the same areas, the Common Murre tends to arrive earlier and manages to obtain the choicest nesting platforms, forcing the Thick-billed Murres to the fringes of the combined colony and to the narrowest of the nesting ledges. However, where Common Murres are absent, these wider sites are fully utilized by the Thick-bills.

The two species also differ somewhat in their foraging tendencies, with the Thick-billed consuming a significantly higher percentage of invertebrates than the Common Murre, which eats more fish. Minor differences in body structure suggest that the Thick-billed is better adapted for long-distance flights to and from foraging areas.

Of the two puffins, the Tufted is somewhat larger than the Horned, and the two species overlap over approximately half of their combined nesting ranges. They differ greatly in their nesting ecologies. Tufted Puffins typically dig their own nest cavities in steep, grass-covered slopes and cliff edges, whereas Horned Puffins nest exclusively in natural, rocky crevices. In the Pribilofs, where rocky crevices are more abundant than suitable burrowing sites, the Horned Puffin will nest in crevices too small for the Tufted Puffin.

The two puffin species have similar foraging ecologies, although various studies suggest that there are minor differences in daily foraging periods, choice of foraging areas, foods consumed by adults, and the kinds of prey brought back to nestlings. Their breeding seasons differ by a few weeks, which may further reduce competition during the critical chick-rearing period.

Perhaps the most fascinating of the auks on the Pribilofs are the auklets, which collectively number about a half-million birds, more than half of which are Least Auklets. Vast flocks of these tiny alcids leave and return to their talus nesting slopes at least twice each day, producing clouds of birds that take one's breath away by their size and the erratic nature of their flight.

All of these auklet species, including the Whiskered Auklet (*Aethia pygmea*), not present on the Pribilofs, are crevice-nesters, and thick talus slopes closely adjacent to the coastline provide the optimum breeding habitat. Of these four species, the Parakeet is the largest, and the Crested, Whiskered, and Least are ecologically segregated from one another, since each species tends to nest in rock crevices only slightly larger than the minimum needed to enter and exit.

These nesting tendencies probably also reduce the chance of the nesting birds or their eggs being dug out by Arctic Foxes, which often destroy such burrow-nesting species as the similarly sized Cassin's Auklet (*Ptychorhamphus aleuticus*).

Auklets also exhibit some remarkable variations in their head plumage and bill structures. The plumage differences may help members of a species recognize one another during courtship, while the bill differences help not only with species recognition but also with foraging specialization.

In the Pribilofs area, the Crested Auklet has been found to concentrate on larger marine amphipods as a major food resource, while the Parakeet Auklet feeds on a wider variety of invertebrates which are generally smaller than those taken by the Crested. The tiny Least Auklet concentrates on a number of small planktonic invertebrates.

Like their large relatives, the puffins, auklets molt a substantial section of their beak covering after the nesting season, suggesting that these beak features are significant aspects of species recognition and courtship behavior.

Remarkably little is known of the courtship and mating

behavior of auklets, because it probably occurs while the birds are at sea and might be continued at their nest cavities. What little is known suggests that a prolonged monogamous pair-bond occurs. Both members return to the same nesting cavity year after year, facilitating the reunion of birds with their former mates.

Auklets, and probably all other members of this family, engage in prolonged mutual billing, nibbling, or preening of the head region, apparently as a primary pair-forming or pair-maintaining display. This concentration of courtship activity in the head and bill region helps to explain why nearly all closely related members of the family are similar in their general body plumage but are recognizably different in their bill and head characteristics.

In this family, the sexes are identical in plumage and virtually so in their vocalizations. Therefore, species and sexual recognition mechanisms must be incorporated into their behavioral signaling systems. It appears that some calls and postures, especially those indicating hostility or social dominance, are performed either exclusively or much more frequently by males, which may help them determine one another's sex.

All told, the Pribilof Islands and their seabirds are still relatively secure from external threats of human disturbance, potential overharvesting of the marine food chains, and pollution.

There is some potential, if limited, for development of tourism in the Pribilofs, but only the hardiest and most enthusiastic of bird-watchers are willing to assume the cost and risk the uncertain air service, often dismal weather, and rather Spartan accommodations now available to visitors. For the lucky few who do reach the islands and are able to spend days on end surrounded by some of the most spectacular views of seabirds and wildlife found anywhere in the world, the Pribilof Islands are a vision of a nearly unspoiled and fragile paradise, for which any major changes could only be for the worse.

III. *Sky*

MIGRATIONS OF
THE IMAGINATION

The Gifts of the Cranes

Sandhill Crane calling

THERE IS A WONDERFUL OLD TRADITION IN SOME parts of Scandinavia in which the children hang their stockings outside their houses during those days in early spring when the European cranes first return from their wintering areas in France and Spain. Sometimes the children may place an ear of corn or some other gift to pass on to the cranes, whose welcome voices and overhead flocks are the surest sign of spring and renewed hope for the future after enduring a long, unbearably dark, and frigid Scandinavian winter. In return, the birds may leave a gift of their own for the children before they pass still farther northward to their remote subarctic breeding grounds. It's a tradition I would love to see started in North America, perhaps as a substitute for what I regard as the rather silly Easter bunny–Easter egg tradition. As an ornithologist I have a good deal of trouble thinking that even children can believe that rabbits might actually produce and deliver dyed bird eggs or their candy versions. Yet I think it was no less a personage than the White Queen who admitted that she liked to think of at least six impossible things before breakfast, and so egg-bearing rabbits are perhaps better than everyday television in enriching the imaginary lives of children.

Speaking of unbelievable things, it is unbelievable that so many Nebraskans have yet to make what is for me an annual religious pilgrimage to the Platte Valley each spring, to revel in the sounds and sights of uncountable cranes and geese, and to know that the promise of another Nebraska spring has been fulfilled by their simple presence. The splendor of several thousand cranes flying up and down the river as nightfall approaches, all looking for a safe sandbar on which to spend the night, and with the juvenile birds calling constantly in their distinctive baby voices to remain in touch with their parents in the fading light, touches one's soul at so many levels that it is hard not to weep from the utter magic and power of it all. After every such experience I am as emotionally

Sky drained as I am after hearing a perfect performance of a Beethoven symphony, or a sacred Bach composition. The word "religion" comes from the Latin word *religio,* meaning a bond between humans and the gods, and in common with the enduring orchestral music, cranes provide that connection perfectly. Often appearing miraculously from incredible heights like celestial seraphim, and sometimes similarly ascending into the sky until they are lost to human view, our Sandhill Cranes are every bit as wondrous as the angels painted on the ceiling of the Sistine Chapel, and one does not have to travel to Italy to appreciate them.

All wonderful and rare things in this world carry a significant price tag; otherwise they would be neither rare nor so highly valued. The price tag on our cranes is simply this: we must be willing to protect from destruction the wonderful river that crosses Nebraska like a beautiful quicksilver necklace, the Platte River. Beyond its rich historic value, the Platte is easily the most valuable and most threatened of our surface waters. It is a river that millions of bison once drank from, and one along which tens of thousands of immigrants once passed on their way to building a complete America. Wading in that graceful river is like wading into history; it is a river that offers many quiet gifts to us. Yet these are also rich gifts that we must be willing to protect, cherish, and finally pass on to our children as if they were our collective family's greatest treasures, which in fact they are.

I offered such a gift recently, when for the first time I took my seven-year-old granddaughter to see the Sandhill Cranes on the Platte. She had been asking me to take her for several years: indeed, ever since her mother explained that the cranes I spent so much time watching each year weren't the kind of machinery cranes she already knew about. This year, armed with a pair of binoculars and the knowledge garnered by reading a children's book on cranes, she was finally ready.

This March, like unnumbered Marches before it, the cranes

have again returned to the Platte Valley. Their annual predictable appearance is like watching a favorite spring flower unfolding, a piece of music developing, a promise being fulfilled. That promise is being paid annually by the experienced migrant cranes to all the generations of cranes that have stopped in the Platte Valley in eons past. The present generation must instill among the less experienced birds a firm memory of the Platte, the locations of its wet meadows, its abundant grainfields, and a collective memory of its gentle evenings, when the river's cool waters lap at the feet of the cranes as they stand all night in shallow waters around the edges of the Platte's innumerable sandbars and islands.

The sights and sounds of cranes roosting on the Platte are immeasurably old, but are also forever new and variable. Early one March morning, as night slowly gave rise to dawn on the Platte River, the planet Mars was high in the sky, Venus was brilliant in the eastern sky, and the moon was approaching fullness. Great Horned Owls sang occasional duets, and the cranes talked to one another with increasing urgency. Then, just before sunrise, the cranes rose majestically in flock after flock, along with even larger groups of Canada Geese, and headed toward feeding grounds south of the river. To one who has never experienced the visual and aural components of such a scene, it is nearly impossible to try to convey, but standing beside railroad tracks as a speeding locomotive passes by may give some slight idea of the sound and implicit power expressed in the takeoff of ten thousand cranes.

I once described the music of crane calls as perhaps being most like that of angels singing, but on further thought I believe that this is an unfair comparison. Angel choruses, judging from most paintings one sees, seem to be highly age- or sex-biased in favor of young attractive females, whereas the music of crane flocks exhibits all the democratic exuberance imaginable when every bird, regardless of sex and age, is calling simultaneously at full voice regardless of pitch. Crane

Sky chorusing can only remind one of the final movement of Beethoven's Ninth Symphony, as chaotically sung by a vast assemblage of tone-deaf but enthusiastic lovers of fine music.

The evening return by the cranes to the river near sunset each day is not so much a sudden explosion as a gradual buildup of tension and beauty, in a manner resembling Ravel's *Bolero*. As the western skies redden the cranes fly up and down the main channel of the river, calling with gradually increasing urgency, evidently trying to make the decision as to where they might most safely spend their night. Sometimes the weak, chirping voice of a yearling crane, seemingly worried about possibly being separated from its parents in the evening confusion, penetrates the general level of crane conversation. The decision to land is finally made by a few adventuresome souls, and the rest of the birds tumble in behind, all calling at the top of their lungs. Watching this incredibly boisterous activity, my granddaughter turned to me and asked, "Grampa, do the cranes do this only on Saturdays?" Gradually, as twilight descends into night, the noise level of roosting flocks dies down. Yet all night long some cranes in every flock remain awake and stand watch while others sleep with their bills tucked under their wings, the latter presumably secure in the knowledge that some of their group are always alert and watching for danger.

These unspoken promises, both daily and annual, that the cranes keep with one another and with the river remind us of our individual promises and personal obligations to ourselves, our kin, and our land. Holding the hand of a small grandchild, as a flock of cranes passes overhead, and telling her that if she is very lucky she might also one day show these same sights to her own grandchild are a powerful lesson in faith, hope, and love. And beauty, touched by love, is somehow transformed into magic.

OPPOSITE PAGE:
Male Spectacled Eider in flight

Flight of the Sea Ducks

NESTING IN COLONIES THAT CAN NUMBER HUNDREDS of birds, the eiders are among the most conspicuous of tundra-breeding ducks. Although female eiders are a study in grays and browns that match the arctic tundra, the males are most boldly patterned in black and white, with striking green head colors. When the nesting season ends, the birds disperse over the vastness of the northern oceans, out of range of most human observers. Of the four species of eiders, the two most abundant and largest have circumpolar breeding distributions and extensive marine wintering ranges. These are the Common Eider (*Somateria mollissima*) and the King Eider (*S. spectabilis*), whose flesh, eggs, and feathers have played a role in the survival of high-latitude human populations for thousands of years, and whose down has insulating qualities that are yet to be matched by artificially manufactured substitutes. The other two eider species are smaller and have much more restricted breeding distributions that center on the Bering Sea. These are the Spectacled Eider (*S. fischeri*), named for the gogglelike feathering pattern around its eyes, and the Steller's Eider (*Polysticta stelleri*), named in honor of G. W. Steller, the naturalist on Bering's ill-fated expedition to Alaska.

Steller's Eider breeds almost entirely in Siberia and winters

Sky primarily along the coastlines of the Aleutian Islands and in the vicinity of the Kamchatka Peninsula and the adjacent Kuril Islands. The Spectacled Eider, which nests commonly in some parts of eastern Siberia and in the Kuskokwim Delta of Alaska, seems to disappear into the open spaces of the Bering Sea every fall and is not seen again until the breakup of ice along the coasts of Siberia and Alaska the following spring.

It is the relatively sudden spring appearance of vast flocks of eiders, as the pack ice begins to break up near shore, that provides one of the intriguing aspects of these sea ducks. The flocks appear every spring at points and headlands along the western and northern Alaska coasts in numbers that are simply staggering. At places like Cape Romanzof and Cape Prince of Wales on the western coast of Alaska, flocks of eiders can be observed passing overhead in almost endless northbound streams in May and early June.

On his trip to Alaska's Yukon-Kuskokwim Delta in 1924, naturalist Herbert Brandt watched the eider migration across Point Dall and Cape Romanzof. There the sequence of spring arrival was evidently associated with body size; the relatively large Common Eider arriving about the first week of May, followed in a few days by flocks of the King Eider. The smaller Spectacled Eider and the Steller's Eider followed in that order. One flight, predominantly of King Eiders, began late in the afternoon of May 14, apparently continued all night, and persisted all of the next day. Brandt considered the number of birds passing over Point Dall and Cape Romanzof on May 15 as "beyond all comprehension." Nonetheless, he provided an estimate of 75,000 for a two- to three-hour period on that day. Essentially all of these were full-plumaged adult birds, indicating that as many or more first-year immatures must have remained at sea during the summer. The younger birds rarely come within sight of land until their second spring of life.

At the time of Brandt's expedition, three of the four eider species nested in the vicinity of Hooper Bay, with the Spec-

tacled and Steller's Eiders the most common. The Steller's
Eider has apparently ceased to breed in that vicinity, and its
wintering population has dropped from about 200,000 birds
to 30,000–65,000 by 1991. The Spectacled Eider's population
has plummeted in recent years as well, and this area is the
center of the species' breeding range in North America.

On a visit to the Hooper Bay area in 1963, I observed that
the Spectacled Eiders were nesting nearly colonially, with nests
often within fifty feet of their neighbors. Within a week or
two after the females had begun their incubation, the males
returned to the open sea. Based on observations by E. W.
Nelson in the late 1800s, it is possible that the male North
American Spectacled Eiders fly more than 200 miles north,
to the vicinity of Norton Sound, in late June or early July to
undergo a postbreeding molt.

All four species of eiders are known to undertake such "molt
migrations," which can be of remarkable length. For example,
a substantial number of male Steller's Eiders from breeding
populations in eastern Siberia have been banded at Izembek
Bay, Alaska, where they undergo postbreeding molt. Some
of these banded birds have been recovered from points as
far away as the Lena Delta in Siberia, nearly 2,000 miles to
the west.

Why birds would migrate so far prior to undergoing the
physiological stresses associated with molting can only be explained if the destination offers an unusual degree of safety
and food. This is indeed the case. The shallow and plant-rich
waters of Izembek and Bechevin Bays on the Alaska Peninsula provide an abundance of aquatic life sufficient to sustain
some 200,000 eiders at one time. The molting Steller's Eiders, which include not only males but also some females that
presumably were unsuccessful in their nesting effort, remain
in the vicinity of Izembek Bay from fall through April.

The molt migrations of King Eiders are also impressive.
The North American population breeds along the northern

coastline of Alaska and Canada and falls into two groups: those that fly directly west across the north coastline of Alaska to a destination that is probably in the vicinity of Point Lay, about 200 miles southwest of Point Barrow; and those that fly almost directly east to the coast of Greenland. Virtually entire migratory flocks are composed of males, including both adults and immatures. The concentration off Greenland numbers several hundred thousand birds and includes all of the birds from Canada's eastern Arctic, thus requiring a flight, in some instances, of more than 1,500 miles.

The King Eider populations of Victoria Island and of Canada's western Arctic may number at least a million birds. Nearly all of these pass by Point Barrow between mid-July and the end of August. This is evidently a migratory tradition of long standing, for among the most common weapons excavated at Point Barrow are 900- to 1,400-year-old Eskimo bone and ivory bola weights used in hunting eiders.

The first of the massive flocks to pass over Point Barrow in July is composed entirely of adult males; but by mid-August there is a preponderance of unsuccessful female nesters. The later molting period of the females allows them more time to complete a nesting cycle. At least some of the adult females that succeed in hatching young do not participate in any of the major flights to the molting grounds; instead they remain until their young fledge in late August, then undergo their molt on the breeding grounds. By forming crèches, relatively few females are required to remain on the breeding grounds with the flightless young, thus freeing the rest for their molting migration.

After the adult eiders have finished molting, they again migrate. The eastern King Eider population moves from western to southern Greenland and the coasts of Labrador and Newfoundland. The Alaskan birds move south to the Pribilof Islands, Saint Lawrence Island, and the Aleutian Islands, where as many as a quarter-million birds may winter.

Little is known of Common Eider migrations in North
America. In Scotland the movement from the breeding
grounds to the molting area is only about 60 miles. In Norway there is enough topographic protection and available food
in the breeding range to allow the completion of the flightless
period there, and no special molt migration pattern has
developed.

While the eiders in Alaska are still on their nesting grounds,
they suffer some depredations from humans. At Hooper Bay
I often observed young Eskimo men collecting waterfowl eggs
and hunting adult eiders with single-shot rifles. Herbert
Brandt, writing of the same area, said that the skins of eiders
and other ducks, and also those of geese, provided the favored lining for parkas, with the feathered side worn against
the face. On Cape Dorset, Eskimo men form organized egg-
collecting forays to the colonies of Common Eiders, while
women and children set up snares to capture nesting females.

In contrast to the harvesting techniques used in Canada
and Alaska, the people of Iceland, Scandinavia, and Siberia
have developed a tradition of eider "farming." In eider farming, down is collected intermittently during each nesting season, without destroying the nests or killing the females. When
the female is approximately halfway through the incubation
period there is a maximum amount of high-quality down
present in the nest, and most of this can be removed without
endangering the eggs. After the eggs have hatched, the remaining mixture of down and breast feathers can be gathered, although this collection is of second-quality and far lower
commercial value. Roughly three-quarters of an ounce of high-
quality down can be collected per nest, plus an equivalent
amount of poorer-quality down.

In Norway and Iceland the birds have been protected so
long that they are almost domesticated. They are protected
from predators and provided with specially prepared nesting
sites. Colonies of more than 5,000 pairs have been developed

under such conditions. On some eider farms the eggs are also taken from the first clutch, forcing the female to renest and produce a new clutch that she is allowed to hatch. In Russia, eider-down collection has been a part of the northern economy for centuries; seventeenth-century documents mention "bird down" among the goods sold to Dutch merchants. In 1930 about 1,000 pounds of down were obtained from Novaya Zemlya; on some protected areas of this archipelago, the density of nesting birds has increased to as much as 13,000 nests per hectare (2.47 acres).

Once the birds have left their breeding grounds and moved to molting or wintering areas, their foraging activities and ecological relationships become progressively obscure. The three largest eiders have virtually identical bill structures, which can be characterized as being relatively massive, with a broad and flattened nail-like structure at the tip, much like that of their near relatives the scoter ducks. The larger eiders and scoters (*Melanitta* spp.) are known to feed predominantly on mollusks, particularly such bivalves as blue mussels, probably the single most important food of Common Eiders. King Eiders also feed to a great extent on mussels, but are believed to forage in somewhat deeper waters and to utilize a greater proportion of echinoderms such as sand dollars and sea urchins in their diet. In spite of its lack of obvious streamlining or other diving adaptations, the King Eider is able to dive to great depths to forage, reportedly as deep as 180 feet. This allows the species to forage farther from shore than the other eiders or scoters and reduce foraging competition between them.

Far less is known of the foraging ecology of Spectacled Eiders in their wintering or migratory areas. Indications are that the Spectacled Eider also feeds on bivalve mollusks. Since it is scarcely seen near any coastlines in winter, the implication is that the Spectacled Eider must be able to dive to considerable depths in order to obtain its food.

The Steller's Eider is known to forage in relatively shallow waters, often feeding while wading at the water's edge, dab- bling like surface-feeding ducks. They evidently prefer soft- bodied crustaceans, such as amphipods and isopods, over mollusks, and in correlation with this, their bills have soft, membranous edges and an inconspicuous bill nail that is ill-suited to scraping bivalve mollusks off rocks. Consequently, the Steller's Eider competes little for forage with other eiders.

The breeding biology and molting and wintering migra-tions of the eiders have gradually brought them into increas-ing contact with humans, if only for a month or so each year. To the people of the northern latitudes, eiders have been a valuable resource because of those characteristics of their life cycle that seasonally bring the birds in to shore on the remote coastlines of Alaska and Canada. For the rest of us, the eiders must mostly remain elusive and mysterious seabirds, nearly as mythical as mermaids, calling us to gaze at the maps of arctic America and wish that we could someday make ren-dezvous with them on some wild stretch of arctic tundra.

*Trumpeter Swan
in flight*

The Triumphant Trumpeters

LARGEST OF ALL THE SWANS AND HEAVIEST OF NORTH
American birds, the Trumpeter Swan (*Cygnus buccinator*) is
on the increase. Once common and widespread over much of
the western United States, the bird was a winter resident of
the lower reaches of the Mississippi Valley, Louisiana, and
Texas. During the last century, however, trade in swanskins—
used to make powder puffs and writing and drawing quills—
and the sale of eggs to collectors had a heavy impact on the
species. In the period from 1853 to 1877, for example, London
sales of Trumpeter swanskins imported through the Hudson's
Bay Company totaled nearly 18,000, an average of about 750
per year. Destruction of their prairie habitat and increased
disturbance also took a heavy toll on these shy birds. By the
time the species came under the complete protection of the
Migratory Bird Treaty Act in 1918, many ornithologists believed that the species was doomed to extinction.

Population surveys in the early 1930s gave estimates of from
37 to 97 surviving Trumpeter Swans, nearly all of them in
Yellowstone National Park and the nearby Red Rock Lakes
area in southwestern Montana. At that time, a large breeding
population in Alaska was overlooked because it was believed

Sky that those birds were Whistling Swans, a species closely related to the Trumpeters. Since the realization in 1954 that Trumpeter Swans nested in Alaska, surveys have indicated that a very large and secure population exists in that state.

But in the 1930s, conservationists did not know how many birds existed north of the Canadian border, and the outlook for the species within the contiguous United States was grim. The establishment of Red Rock Lakes Migratory Waterfowl Refuge in southwestern Montana in 1935 was certainly the most significant factor in protecting the last remnant of breeding Trumpeter Swans south of Canada. The nucleus of birds at that refuge provided other parks and refuges with Trumpeters to establish new flocks. The first such transplant was conducted in 1938, when four cygnets were placed on the National Elk Refuge, near Jackson, Wyoming. Six additional birds were released there in 1939 and 1941, and the first breeding occurred in 1944. Thereafter, nesting took place nearly every year, although no more than two nests were reported in any single year.

Presumably from these nestings, Trumpeter Swans colonized abutting Grand Teton National Park a few years after its establishment in 1950. (The protection from disturbance by ranching and other related activities formerly in the area probably made colonization possible.)

One of the first areas to be occupied in the Tetons was Christian Pond, a thirty-acre marsh near Jackson Lake Lodge. Breeding occurred on that pond as early as 1954, and nesting attempts were made every year since, at least into the 1980s. During the eight-year period from 1969 through 1976, at least eighteen cygnets were raised by a single pair using Christian Pond. Whether the same pair was involved every year is not certain, but it is possible: swans are long-lived; some have survived in captivity for more than thirty years, including a Trumpeter Swan that lived more than thirty-two years.

Other areas in the park have also been used by Trumpeter
Swans for nesting. In the six-year period between 1970 and
1975 a total of eight different sites had nests. Yet during that
entire period only forty-three cygnets are known to have been
reared, including those from Christian Pond. Considering that
the usual clutch is four to six eggs, the reproductive success of
the seven known pairs in the park each year was extraordi-
narily low; the average for all pairs was less than one young
successfully raised per year.

Trumpeter Swans have now been breeding in Grand Teton
National Park for at least forty years; yet the number of breeding pairs has not increased measurably in the last twenty years.
The question that arises is: What could be responsible for
this bird's low reproductive rate and nonincreasing population in the park?

The reproductive potential of the Trumpeter Swan is typical of swans in general and might be considered a model for
large waterfowl. Although some refuge-raised Trumpeters
have bred when they were approaching the end of their third
year, wild birds often do not breed until their fourth year as a
result of competition for suitable nest sites with older and
already established pairs. Thereafter, the birds attempt to nest
every year for as long as they live. In growing populations the
percentage of young in the fall is about 25–40 percent, or about
3–3.5 cygnets per brood. The survival rate for Trumpeter Swans
in the wild is still unknown, but in the related Bewick's race
of the Tundra Swan (*Cygnus columbianus bewickii*) of Eurasia,
it is about 85 percent per year. Likewise, the Eurasian Whooper
Swan, sometimes considered to be the same species as the
Trumpeter, has an estimated annual survival rate of 83 percent. The potential longevity of Trumpeter Swans should result in a large number of offspring over their lifetimes. Why,
then, is Grand Teton National Park not afloat in Trumpeter
Swans?

Sky To answer that question, one must examine not only the environment in terms of its carrying capacity for swans but also the efficiency of the swans' reproductive efforts.

Studies on the biology of Trumpeter Swans indicate that their reproductive needs are fairly simple. Territories of breeding pairs are almost always large to insure an adequate food supply for the adults and as many as six young. Rarely is a territory established on a pond or lake of less than five acres, and in Grand Teton National Park, as well as at Red Rock Lakes Refuge, the average territorial size is about thirty acres. Some marshes or small lakes as large as one hundred acres may be defended from intrusion by other pairs, particularly if the shoreline is open enough for unobscured vision. Both the white plumage and the extremely loud vocalization of the Trumpeter Swan have apparently evolved as devices for proclaiming large territories by maximizing individual conspicuousness.

Other considerations besides a minimum water area are important in determining what constitutes acceptable nesting habitat. First, water levels should be stable, avoiding the possibility of the nest's exposure to territorial predators as a result of dropping levels or of flooding caused by a rise in water level. Second, much or all of the water in a territory should be from one to three feet deep, to allow for subsurface foraging while swimming, and the water should be quiet and wave-free, with an abundance of emergent, floating, and submerged plants. The emergent plants are primarily of value as cover and as foundation material for the nest, while the submerged and floating plants provide an adequate food supply for these large herbivores.

Given these considerations, that Grand Teton National Park does not have more nesting swans is not surprising. Many of its waters are deep, clear lakes, formed by glacial action, that offer little food or cover for the birds. Christian Pond, however, as well as several of the other regular nesting sites in the park, is beaver formed, and its level is controlled by beaver dams. As with the moose, which feeds extensively on aquatic plants, and the Greater Sandhill Crane, which nests in or around beaver impoundments, the presence of Trumpeter Swans in Grand Teton National Park is closely tied to the abundance and distribution of beavers.

A very high mortality of eggs or cygnets is the probable reason for the low reproductive rates. To avoid overestimating cygnet production, the National Park Service's annual count of swan families in the park is usually made in late August or early September, when the young birds are nearly fledged. Therefore, there has been no way of knowing if most mortality occurs prior to hatching or sometime thereafter. But during three summers spent in the park, I never saw a full brood of six cygnets and rarely saw more than two, even shortly after hatching. This would suggest that most mortality happens early, probably before the young are one to two weeks old. In any attempt to understand what the cause of such cygnet or egg mortality might be, the breeding logistics for a bird the size of a Trumpeter Swan have to be considered.

Trumpeter Swans typically build large, mounded nests in marshes, well away from shore, in water about one to two feet deep. These nests are often constructed of bulrushes, cattails, or other emergent vegetation; at times beaver lodges or muskrat houses are also used. A week or more may be spent building a new nest or refurbishing an old foundation. Egg-laying then begins and continues for 10 days until a full clutch has been deposited. Incubation begins with the last egg and lasts an average of 36 to 40 days. Finally, the young birds have an extremely long fledging period, estimated at from 91 to 122 days in the Montana-Wyoming population. Thus, a minimum of 142 days, and perhaps as much as 173 days, are required from the time nest construction begins until the young

Sky fledge. Since the frost-free period in the Grand Teton National Park area is less than 80 days, the bird's long reproductive cycle poses certain risks: the eggs might be fatally chilled before they hatch; the young cygnets might freeze before they develop adequate temperature regulation; and the water might freeze over before the juveniles fledge and thus lose their vulnerability to coyotes and other predators.

I believe this environmental factor is primarily responsible for the low reproductive success of Trumpeter Swans in the Grand Teton area. Originally adapted to breeding on prairie marshes in areas where the frost-free period is often 200 days or longer, Trumpeters often succumb under the severe strains of breeding in montane areas. Even in southeastern Alaska, where the largest population of Trumpeter Swans now exists, the frost-free period is more than 120 days and thus far less likely to be a mortality factor. In Alaska, 80 to 85 percent of the cygnets survive at least to the age of two months.

If there is a lesson to be learned from this, it is that future releases of Trumpeter Swans into refuges should be done with some attention to the climatic characteristics of the area. A release in 1960 at Lacreek National Wildlife Refuge in South Dakota has been among the most successful of the Trumpeter transplants; the population there increased to several hundred birds, and the swans have spread out and nested in many counties of South Dakota and several in Nebraska. Successful releases have also been made (since 1966) in Minnesota, where the species is now well established, with about 350 birds. Releases have also been made in Ontario (1982), Michigan (1986), Wisconsin (1987), and Ohio (1995).

As of 1995, there were nearly 20,000 Trumpeter Swans in North America, a record high total. Of these nearly 16,000 were in southern and central Alaska, about 800 were in Canada, and about 400 were in the Rocky Mountains south of Canada. The Pacific coast population of Alaska and Brit-

ish Columbia has nearly doubled during the past ten years,
and seems to show no sign of stabilizing yet. Almost 1,000
swans were present by 1995 in the High Plains and Mississippi Flyway, with Minnesota a major population center.
Without doubt, many other refuges in the Great Plains could
support breeding populations of this magnificent bird once
its traditional breeding habitat—the remaining marshlands
of the Great Plains, not some semifrozen mountain lake—is
recognized.

The 6,000-mile Odyssey of a Globe-trotting Bird

IT WAS EARLY JULY, AND THROUGHOUT THE tundra near Churchill, in northeastern Manitoba, shorebirds were hatching, the downy young quickly disappearing into thick cover with their parents. I had been watching the nests of several different species, trying to photograph youngsters for a forthcoming book on the world's shorebirds. But I still lacked photos of American Golden-Plover (*Pluvialis dominica*) chicks. A predator had just destroyed the nest I had been observing. Now the adult birds had to start their family all over again, and I had to find another incubating pair.

One of my colleagues remembered spotting a plover nest alongside a heavily traveled road near town. Despite its exposed location we decided to check its hatching status and assess the adults' tolerance of people.

At the nest site we easily found the incubating female on the sparse and stony tundra. As I walked up to the nest her mate whistled a warning note in the distance; she crouched instantly. I stood near the nest for several minutes before she moved away and I was able to see that the eggs had already started to hatch. The timing was perfect. In addition, and perhaps more important, the female seemed remarkably tame.

Sky I would be able to get the photos I wanted from this nest within a day or two.

It wasn't long before we discovered what was probably the cause of her fearlessness. I had no sooner rejoined my colleague when a car screeched to a halt behind us. Out stepped a portly woman, clutching a plastic bag full of bread crumbs. With a cheery "Hello, darling" to the plover, she dumped the bag's contents a few inches from the bird's bill, then turned to leave.

After recovering from my initial surprise, I asked the woman why she was feeding the plover bread, since they forage almost exclusively on animal material. With a somewhat condescending smile she replied, "Oh, it's quite all right. I bring out bread to the little dear every day, and by the next day it's completely gone, so I'm sure she loves it." With that, she quickly got back into her car and disappeared in the direction of town.

As soon as the woman left, the plover began to pick up the larger bread crumbs one at a time, fly off with them for a short distance, and drop them into the tundra vegetation. Taking pity on the bird, I helped her clear away the mess and then sat down a few yards away to watch the late stages of incubation.

Like all birds that nest in the Arctic region, plovers are severely bothered by mosquitoes and other insects that bite them around the eyes and the base of the bill, where feathers are short or lacking. Many larger species, such as ducks and geese, simply sit and accept the constant onslaught, but this alert female would have no part of such foolishness. With a sudden movement she would dislodge each mosquito as soon as it landed on her head, catch it while it was still floundering in midair, and swallow it.

The nesting pair had chosen a patch of andromeda and arctic rhododendron—tiny tundra flowers—in which to conceal their eggs. When huddled down, the female protruded above the ground no more than did the rounded rocks strewn widely about the slope. Indeed, the gold spangles on her back seemed to mimic the yellow lichen-covered rocks, just as the eggs were marvelously scrawled with blackish markings to blend into the stony background. Only the black plumage of her undersides, visible when she sat erect, revealed the nest's location.

The golden-plover's dark plumage is a curious reversal of countershading—a form of protective coloring seen in many ground-nesting birds and other animals. In this type of camouflage, the animal's light undersides are shadowed from above by the sun, making the creature appear uniformly dark and thus less conspicuous. Scientists have suggested that light underparts would not be effective in Arctic-nesting birds, inasmuch as the low angle of the sun at high latitudes does not cast enough of a shadow.

Another Arctic nester, the slightly larger Black-bellied Plover (*P. squatarola*), also has a black neck and chest, but it has a white rump and its upper body is much grayer than that of the golden. This is probably a camouflaging adaptation to the species' more northerly nesting range on very dry tundra, so rich in grayish-white lichens. The downy chicks of both species are mottled with black and bright gold on their upper parts—again apparently to mimic the tundra background.

The American Golden-Plover and Black-bellied Plover are among the most widely traveled shorebirds of the world. Each summer they nest in the arctic regions of the Northern Hemisphere and each winter they migrate about 6,000 miles to southern South America to take advantage of the austral summer. Most golden-plovers spend the winter on the grassy pampas of northern Argentina and Uruguay, but the species has at times been seen as far south as Isla Grande, Tierra del Fuego. By contrast, the Black-bellied Plover travels farther north to nest and usually winters along both coasts of South America, but only as far south as Brazil and northern Chile.

Sky Golden-plovers are monogamous; the adults migrate together and land at the nesting areas already paired. Evidently they find mates during their second year of life, probably while still on their wintering grounds. In late March large flocks leave the pampas for eastern Peru—the first leg of their long spring journey.

From there they fly 2,000 miles to Texas, apparently nonstop since there are few records of them occurring in Central America during spring. They gradually work their way north over the Great Plains; some reach the Canadian border by about the end of April. Finally, in mid-May, they begin to arrive in the Churchill area along the shoreline of Hudson Bay, with the majority completing the trek between May 25 and June 5.

To take advantage of the all-too-brief arctic summer the plovers must select nest sites as soon as the tundra becomes snow-free. Males quickly begin their territorial displays, flying in wide circles above the thawing tundra, calling and coursing about with exaggerated wingbeats. Such activities normally scatter the pairs, although the nest I was watching sat no more than seventy yards from the next one. This represented unusually close nest building: The incubating birds could certainly see one another, but they showed no signs of hostility at this late stage of the breeding cycle.

In some parts of the tundra the egg-laying process begins as early as June 11, but most eggs are laid in the last two weeks of that month. Like nearly all North American shorebirds, golden-plovers generally lay four eggs and always arrange them with the pointed end facing into the center of the nest. In this manner the clutch takes up minimal space and the eggs have maximum surface contact, presumably for the greatest heat maintenance.

The female usually deposits her eggs at the rate of one per day, and they are left untended until the clutch is complete. Since the nest consists merely of a depression in the tundra vegetation, the adults must supply continuous body heat to incubate the eggs. As soon as the egg is laid, the parents begin sitting on the nest; incubation takes about 26 days.

Although both parents take turns, the females seem to spend more time incubating, while the males maintain vigilance from a short distance. Should a person or a predator come too close to the nest, whichever bird is sitting on the eggs performs a broken-wing act, dragging its wings and uttering pathetic-sounding cries, to draw the intruder away. Occasionally both adults engage in this behavior simultaneously, but usually it is the female, while the slightly larger male stands nearby endlessly screaming.

After a chick first pips, or pierces, its shell, hatching time varies among different bird species, often taking several days for some shorebirds. Nevertheless, hatching of the entire plover brood is synchronous—all the young emerge within a four-to-six-hour period.

When they finally burst free of their shells they are wet and wobbly, obviously exhausted. But a single hour transforms them into dry and fluffy little creatures, scampering around trying to peer out from under their mother's breast as she tries all the harder to keep them from view. As soon as all the chicks have hatched, the brooding parent picks up the larger shell fragments, flies off with them one at a time, and drops them onto the tundra, probably to hide the nest site from predators. Quite possibly the female's earlier response to the white bread crumbs was simply a slightly misdirected version of this protective behavior.

Plover chicks are well developed upon hatching and within about a day are foraging for mosquitoes, beetles, and other insects. Their parents never have to offer them food. Soon the family leaves the nest site, abandoning any infertile or otherwise unhatched eggs. Both parents, however, stay with their brood and help protect them until they have fledged, which takes about three weeks.

Sky Just about the time the young have mastered the art of flying, their parents abandon them for the fall migration. In the Churchill area this begins in mid-August and peaks about the first of September. The exact route taken by the Churchill adults is uncharted, but they probably fly either south around the base of Hudson Bay, or directly across the bay, heading for the Atlantic coast. We do now know that the adults assemble in early fall in Labrador, then traverse the Gulf of Saint Lawrence and concentrate in Nova Scotia before flying south over the Atlantic to the Lesser Antilles and the northeastern coast of South America.

This is a hazardous route; we suspect that many birds are lost during fall storms over the Atlantic. Still, most arrive safely on their wintering grounds by the end of September.

On the other hand, all the young birds and some adults journey south by a safer and far less arduous route. They remain behind for several weeks, gathering and foraging on the tundra and nearby beaches. In September they gradually move down across the Great Plains states, reaching the Gulf of Mexico by the end of the month. From there they slowly make their way over Central America and the western coast of South America, probably landing in Peru and Chile by October or November. During this time they no doubt mingle with many other migratory shorebirds, like Black-bellied Plovers and Stilt Sandpipers.

Curiously, the Pacific Golden-Plover (*P. fulva*), a close relative of the American species that nests in western Alaska, has a different migration pattern.

Together with birds that breed in eastern Asia, the entire population of young and old migrate to Japan, the coast of southeastern Asia, the Philippines, and sometimes even to Australia and New Zealand. One such bird, banded during September by researchers in the Pribilof Islands, off the Alaska coast, was recorded six weeks later on Hokkaido Island, north-

ern Japan, having made an overseas flight of about 2,000 miles.
Assuming that the bird continued on to winter in the Philippines or farther south, its round-trip migration would have
covered close to 15,000 miles.

I left the Churchill area too soon to witness the plovers' fall
departure. In fact, the last time I saw that remarkably tame
female and her brood she was impatiently calling after a lag-
gard chick intent on chasing small insects in the grass. The
other three youngsters were following behind her, while the
male stood guard on a nearby slope.

*Eskimo Curlew
in flight*

Where
Have All the
Curlews Gone?

THE MORNING OF SEPTEMBER 16, 1932, DAWNED GRAY and dismal, with a northeaster in full progress along the coast of Long Island. The night before, Robert Cushman Murphy, the noted authority on coastal and sea birds, and his family had camped near the lighthouse at the tip of Montauk Point. Shortly after daylight four large shorebirds headed in from the direction of the sea and dropped into the vegetation of a hillock near Murphy's tent. Stalking the birds, Murphy could scarcely believe his eyes. They were almost certainly Eskimo Curlews (*Numenius borealis*), a species believed by some to be extinct, and had probably come from the coast of Labrador, where a curlew had been shot two weeks previously near the Strait of Belle Isle. So far as is known, that was the last Eskimo Curlew ever shot on the North American continent, and Murphy's observation was to be the last along the Atlantic coast for nearly thirty years.

Those four remnant birds were following one of the most remarkable migration patterns of all the North American shorebirds. They were representatives of a species once so abundant that flocks on the Labrador coast were reported to be a mile long and nearly as wide. The calls of a distant flock

Sky were said to sound like the wind whistling through a ship's rigging or the jingling of countless sleigh bells. When the birds arrived from central Canada in August, they gorged themselves on the abundant invertebrates and crowberries of the Labrador coast in preparation for the long overseas flight to their wintering areas. If the fall weather was favorable, the birds remained in Newfoundland and Nova Scotia until early September, when they would leave for a nonstop flight to the Lesser Antilles, some 2,000 miles to the south. After a brief layover in the Lesser Antilles, the birds continued south over eastern Brazil and on to Argentina. The majority arrived at their winter quarters by mid-September, concentrating in the grassy pampas south of Buenos Aires.

However, fall storms on the Atlantic coast often affected this schedule and itinerary, forcing the birds to hug the North American shoreline. Large flocks would build up along the Atlantic coast, particularly in Massachusetts, on Long Island, and down through the Middle Atlantic and southern states. (Local hunters in New England called the curlews "dough-birds," apparently because they were so fat and tender.) Under adverse weather conditions, some flocks sought refuge on Bermuda. Westerly winds sometimes drove them far out over the Atlantic, and on rare occasions they would touch down in the British Isles.

Such large assemblages of birds did not go unnoticed by hunters, who ruthlessly slaughtered thousands in Labrador every fall. The Hudson's Bay Company's store at Cartwright was a convenient place to sell the tasty birds, which were marketed in all eastern cities, and it was not unusual for twenty-five or thirty hunters to bring in as many as two thousand curlews in a single day. Individual hunters often shot hundreds, usually by stationing themselves between feeding areas and simply waiting for the birds to pass by. The curlews' favored foraging areas were muddy tidal flats where small mollusks were abundant; these, together with crowberries, seem to have been the bulk of their autumnal foods. The birds were so intent on reaching the tidal flats that they continued to circle even when subjected to steady gunfire.

Such slaughter could not go on indefinitely. Between 1870 and 1880 the birds began to diminish rapidly, and by 1890 they had been practically exterminated on the Labrador coast. In that same year, however, a "cloud" of these curlews was observed on the Magdalen Islands in the Gulf of Saint Lawrence, the last sighting of a large flock anywhere. By 1900 the birds were nearly gone. An ornithologist who visited the Labrador coast in the fall of that year saw only five birds there and could find evidence for only about twelve for the entire area. Eight were seen in the fall of 1912 on the Labrador coast, of which all but one were shot.

Fall hunting was not the only hazard for the birds. Those that survived the long fall migration were also hunted without restriction in the South American wintering areas, although the intensity of hunting there was not nearly so great as in North America.

The Eskimo Curlew's traditional spring migration route was quite different from the fall pattern. By late February or early March the birds left their wintering areas and probably undertook a nonstop flight to the Gulf Coast of the United States. They initially concentrated in the coastal prairies of Texas and Louisiana in early or mid-March and gradually moved northward through the southern Great Plains. They began arriving in Oklahoma in late March, and by early April they were abundant in Kansas, western Missouri, western Iowa, and Nebraska, as well as Oklahoma. These great spring flocks reminded the pioneers of Passenger Pigeons, and the birds were often called "prairie pigeons." They foraged and migrated in vast flocks; in flight these might reach a half-mile in length and a hundred yards or more in width. When feeding in fields they frequently covered areas of forty to fifty acres. The largest flocks assembled during the period of corn

Sky planting, when the birds settled on newly plowed fields or burned-off prairie searching for grasshopper eggs, young grasshoppers, and other insects.

Market hunters from such cities as Saint Louis, Kansas City, and Omaha ravaged these flocks without mercy. Wagons brought from Omaha were literally filled with curlews. When they were shot for sport, the birds were simply dumped wholesale on the prairie, their bodies forming heaps as large as several tons of coal. Here, too, the birds circled in masses so dense that one "could scarcely throw a brick or other missile into [them] without striking a bird," according to Myron Swenk, summarizing the species' decline in the Smithsonian Institution's *Annual Report* for 1915.

By mid-May, the birds were moving out of Nebraska and into eastern South Dakota and adjacent southwestern Minnesota. Nebraska seems to have been their last major spring staging area, for sighting records diminish progressively from South Dakota northward. There is no evidence of the birds stopping in North Dakota or in the Prairie Provinces of Canada. Instead, they apparently left eastern South Dakota in mid-May, made an almost nonstop flight to the Northwest Territories, and reached the vicinity of Great Slave Lake in the latter part of May.

Almost certainly the birds began to spread out widely once they reached the arctic tundra. There is no firm evidence that they nested in Alaska, but small curlews were seen in the late 1800s at Saint Micheal and Cape Lisbourne in middle to late May, and very probably bred near Point Barrow since they were reported there between May 20 and July 6 of 1882, a period encompassing the nesting season.

The few actual records of nests include a clutch of three eggs hatching at Point Lake, Mackenzie, found in mid-June of 1822, and about thirty clutches located near Fort Anderson in northern Mackenzie by R. MacFarlane in mid-June of 1863 and 1864. The nests were well hidden in open tundra, and the

143

WHERE
HAVE
ALL THE
CURLEWS
GONE?

clutch, like that of most shorebirds, consisted of four eggs. The incubation period was probably about four weeks, like that of other curlews, and hatching was reported as early as July 12. Another four weeks was probably needed for the young birds to fledge. By the middle of August the birds were ready to begin their fall migration. The majority of the birds, presumably the adults, evidently flew eastward across the northern part of Hudson Bay, thus making a direct line for the Labrador coast. A few early-arriving birds that reached Labrador by the middle of August were probably unsuccessful breeders. There was apparently a second migration route down the west coast of Hudson Bay that reached the Atlantic coast via Ontario and the Great Lakes. A few birds also moved southward through the Great Plains, essentially retracing the spring migration route. As in the American Golden-Plover, which has a similar migration route, these may have been young birds. The few fall records for Nebraska suggest that Eskimo Curlews passed through the state in October. One bird shot in Nebraska at that time had a total of thirty-one grasshoppers in its stomach, as well as numerous small berries.

By 1900, sightings of Eskimo Curlews had become so rare that they can almost be individually noted. In Nebraska the last large flock (seventy to seventy-five birds) was observed in Merrick County in April 1900, while other, smaller numbers were seen in York County in 1904 or 1905, and in Madison County in 1909 or 1910. Among the last birds shot were seven (out of a flock of eight) killed in April 1911 in Merrick County, Nebraska. In September 1913 a single bird was shot in Massachusetts. Finally, a lone bird was killed on April 17, 1915, near Norfolk, Nebraska, just a year prior to the signing of the Migratory Bird Treaty, designed to protect and control the hunting of migrating birds. So far as anyone knows, it was the last curlew to be killed in Nebraska, although a group of eight was reported seen near Hastings on April 8, 1926. In 1924 a small flock was seen near Buenos Aires, Argentina, and one

Sky was collected; the next year a single bird was shot in the same location. In 1929 one was killed in Maine. A collector for museums shot one bird in Labrador in 1926, four in 1927, and one in 1932 — the year Murphy saw the four on Long Island. In 1945 two were reportedly seen in late April on Galveston Island, Texas, and another was reported in mid-July 1956 on Folly Island off the South Carolina coast, a rather unlikely time and location. In June 1946, however, there was another sighting on the South Carolina coastline, and in April 1950 a reliable observer near Rockport, Texas, reported seeing a single bird. In September 1964 a specimen was killed on Barbados. Each new record raised hopes for the species, together with fears that the very last bird had just been seen or killed.

The 1945 Galveston Island sighting had been virtually forgotten by 1959, when on March 22 two bird-watchers there saw a small, strange-looking curlew feeding among a group of Long-billed Curlews. After tentatively identifying it as an Eskimo Curlew, they returned with a professional ornithologist, G. H. Williams, who confirmed their identification.

The bird was seen by numerous other observers until April 12, and during the following year a bird was again observed in the same field. In 1961 perhaps the same bird was observed and successfully photographed, and in 1962 the exciting discovery was made that at least three and possibly four curlews were present on Galveston Island.

These Texas sightings added considerably to the hopes that a breeding population might still exist. Countering this optimism was the possibility that at least some of the birds seen may have been the Asian Little Curlew, a very closely related form (some ornithologists suggest it is a different race of the same species) that breeds in eastern Siberia and normally winters in Australia. But since many of the recent sightings were from the Atlantic rather than the Pacific coast, and were mostly within the traditional migratory corridors of the Eskimo Curlew, these suspicions do not appear to have great merit. Nevertheless, the early sightings of possible breeding birds in western Alaska may indeed have been of the Asian species rather than of the Eskimo Curlew.

There were few sightings in the period between 1965 and the present. In late August 1970, a single bird was reported by two observers at Plymouth Beach, Massachusetts. In early August 1972, two birds were observed closely on Martha's Vineyard, Massachusetts. In mid-August 1976, a pair of probable Eskimo Curlews were seen flying over an area of coastal tundra along the west coast of James Bay by two experienced ornithologists, one of whom had earlier observed the species at Galveston Island. Thus, as recently as twenty years ago there was some evidence that this species, believed by some to have been extinct by 1920, probably still existed. All told, between 1932 and 1976 there have been at least six sightings of the Eskimo Curlew on the coast of Texas, seven from the Atlantic coast, and one from James Bay.

Now, after a period of limited optimism, ornithologists are again in a state of uncertainty and doubt as to the existence of this elusive bird. In spite of the ever-increasing activities of bird-watchers, no sightings have been reported from the Texas coast in the last decade, and the present status of this ill-fated bird is impossible to judge. Most of the persons who have summarized its sad story have come to the conclusion that uncontrolled hunting, particularly spring hunting in the Great Plains, was the single most important factor in its demise. Richard C. Banks of the U.S. National Museum has recently reviewed the history of the species's decline, and although he agrees that hunter overkill was doubtless an important factor, he suggests it may not have been the only one. Several climatic factors, including an increase in fall storms along the North Atlantic coast and possible lowered reproductive success on arctic nesting grounds in the late 1880s during a period of unusually cool summers, could also have contributed to increased mortality and lowered reproductive rates. These

Sky speculations are interesting but inconclusive, and we are left in doubt about what, if anything, can be done to protect and preserve a species that at best seems nearly mythical and at worst may already be extinct.

There must have been a majesty to the swirling flocks of Eskimo Curlews as they swept across the Great Plains or down the Labrador coast. In perpetuating their memory, one can do no better than to quote an early observer, L. M. Turner, who saw a flock of several hundred birds flying south along the Ungava coast of northern Labrador in September 1884:

> *They flew in that peculiar manner which distinguishes the curlews from all other birds in flight, a sort of wedge shape, the sides of which were constantly swaying back and forth like a cloud of smoke wafted by the lightest zephyr. The aerial evolutions of the curlews when migrating are, perhaps, one of the most wonderful in the flight of birds. Long, dangling lines either perpendicular or horizontal, the lower parts of which whirl, rise, or twist spirally, while the apex of the flock is seemingly at rest. At other times the leader plunges downward successively followed by the remainder in most graceful undulation, becoming a dense mass then separating into a thin sheet spread wide; again re-forming into such a variety of positions that no description would suffice.*

The sight of these great shifting clouds of birds, combined with the distant sounds of avian sleigh bells tinkling or wind whistling through a ship's riggings, must have been a magical vision that, like the great herds of bison on the Great Plains, has forever vanished from the American scene.

The Geese from beyond the North Wind

Snow Geese in flight

Sky THE BLUE GOOSE, DESCRIBED IN 1758 BY LINNAEUS on the basis of a drawing of a "blue-winged goose" from the Hudson Bay area and given the name *Anas caerulescens,* has long been a bird of mystery. Each fall enormous flocks would suddenly appear and concentrate in a very small area of coastal Louisiana to spend the winter, then return north and disappear into the wilderness of arctic Canada the following spring. As recently as 1925, Arthur C. Bent summarized the situation, in his famous *Life Histories of North American Birds,* as follows: "To find the breeding resorts of the blue goose is one of the most alluring of the unsolved problems in American ornithology. It is really surprising that such a large and conspicuous species, which is numerically so abundant, can disappear so completely during the breeding season."

The mystery of the Blue Goose's breeding grounds was solved in 1929 by the Canadian ornithologist J. Dewey Soper. After a seven-year search, which covered about 30,000 miles and extended from Hudson Bay to Greenland, he discovered a major nesting colony on Baffin Island. Only a year later, George Sutton, then a Cornell University graduate student, located a second nesting colony on the southern tip of Southampton Island in Hudson Bay, approximately 400 miles from the Baffin Island colony.

Both Soper and Sutton found the smaller race of Snow Geese, or Lesser Snow Geese (aptly named *Chen hyperborea hyperborea,* or "goose from beyond the north wind"), nesting in association with Blue Geese. The Snow Goose, always considered a distinct species, had long been known to nest in the Canadian Arctic, as well as in Greenland and Siberia. Yet on Southampton Island, Sutton found mixed pairs and apparent hybrids between Blue and Lesser Snow Geese. This raised the possibility that the two types were not different species but only subspecies or even minor genetic variants. Despite the evidence provided by the mixed pairs and hybrids, Sutton

concluded that the Lesser Snow and Blue Geese were distinct, although closely related, species. (The larger and high-
arctic-breeding Greater Snow Goose, *Chen caerulescens atlan-*
tica, does not exhibit color phases, and the tiny Ross' Goose,
Chen rossi, exhibits the blue phase only very rarely.)

A few years later, Canadian ornithologist T. H. Manning visited a different nesting colony on Southampton Island, where he found that about half of the Blue Geese were mated to Lesser Snow Geese. Although this percentage of mixed pairs was below that to be expected if the two types were randomly interbreeding (which would prove that the birds were of the same species), it was far more than would be expected if they represented separate species. As a result, he suggested that the two plumage types should be considered as different subspecies. Although the present-day attitude toward bird subspecies is to regard them as geographically separated and morphologically different populations, Manning's recommendation seemed to be the best solution to an otherwise insolvable problem and was gradually adopted.

A solution to the taxonomic dilemma was not forthcoming until the 1940s, when Graham Cooch, then a graduate student at Cornell University, spent several summers studying the breeding biology of Blue and Lesser Snow Geese on Southampton Island. His studies demonstrated that the Blue Goose is only a genetically determined color morph or "phase" of the Lesser Snow Goose, and that both types should be regarded as consisting of only one species, which is now called *Chen caerulescens*. The genetic control determining the two plumage types is a relatively simple one. The factor that prevents massive interbreeding between the two types is a behavioral rather than genetic barrier, and is the result of preferential pairing between birds of the same plumage type.

Cooch also believed that blue and white phases of the Lesser Snow Goose exhibit significant differences in their physiologi-

Sky cal adaptations for breeding. Although no differences were found in nest-site selection or average clutch sizes, white-phase birds were thought by Cooch to normally begin their nesting activities slightly earlier than those of the blue phase. Melting snow and ice at the onset of the breeding season often result in the loss of some of the nests, which are constructed on slight, grassy swells on the tundra. If white-phase birds start nesting sooner, they would be more strongly affected by such losses.

Cooch additionally found that egg predation losses to jaegers and Arctic Foxes tend to be higher during the initial stages of the breeding season. It is possible that, as the snow and ice covering the tundra begin to disappear shortly after the first eggs are laid in late May or early June, depending on the latitude of the colony site, white-phase birds on the nest are more conspicuous to predators. By the same token, the blue-phase birds would be better camouflaged on the muddy ground. The presence of two color phases, then, might serve as a device to keep breeding losses at an acceptable level regardless of weather, while maximizing reproductive efficiency during the limited breeding period (approximately 80 days) typical of arctic climates.

In any case, blue-phase pairs were judged by Cooch to be more successful breeders than white-phase pairs, except when an unusually cold and retarded spring reduces the length of the breeding season. This is likely to be especially disadvantageous to the blue-phase birds if they start breeding later than white-phase individuals.

Because the blue-phase birds are hypothetically favored in relatively mild breeding seasons, the past half-century of climatic amelioration in arctic Canada should have benefited the blue phase and help account for the extension of the breeding range of birds representing this genotype. The blue phase is indeed now found in nesting colonies north and west of

Baffin and Southampton Islands, which previously were entirely composed of white-phase geese, and it is becoming relatively more common in breeding areas where both types traditionally occurred.

Although Cooch's arguments about phase-related differences were compelling and his predictions about future increases in the frequency of blue-phase birds logical, neither of these has proved to be substantiated in recent years. Cooch had predicted that by 1980 most of the Hudson Bay colonies would have a preponderance of blue-phase individuals in their breeding flocks. Although blue-phase birds have increased at those colonies where white-phase birds predominate, in those colonies where blue-phase individuals predominate there has been an increase in white-phase birds. At the intensively studied La Perouse Bay colony near Churchill, Manitoba, the incidence of blue-phase birds increased only from about 20 percent in 1969 to 25 percent by 1981. However, the colony size more than doubled during that period (from 2,000 to 5,500 pairs). More recently it has continued to grow at an amazing rate, and by 1990 contained some 22,500 pairs having a white/blue phase ratio similar to that found in 1981.

Cooch's other hypothesis, that the two color types (now termed "morphs" rather than phases) exhibit different physiological and ecological adaptations for breeding, has also not been confirmed by subsequent research. Studies of the La Perouse Bay colony since 1969 by Dr. Fred Cooke and his colleagues at Queen's College, Ontario, have focused on those aspects of reproductive biology that affect overall productivity (or "net fecundity") of the birds, such as average clutch size, mean brood size at hatching, and overall fledging success. They found no significant differences between the two plumage morphs in any of these and other reproductive components affecting net productivity. They also found no differences in gosling survivorship between the two plumage types among mixed-type offspring of pairs consisting of both plumage morphs. One of Dr. Cooke's associates, Dr. Robert F. Rockwell, was additionally unable to establish any morph-related differences in other aspects affecting longevity and reproductive potential, such as pre-reproductive and adult viability, age of maturation, and relative breeding propensity. He judged that gene flow and assortative mating tendencies (the tendency of birds to preferentially mate with like-type individuals) may serve to explain the persistence and dynamics of the plumage polymorphism now present in Lesser Snow Geese of the La Perouse Bay colony.

Still largely unexplained was how the geese develop strong preferential mating with birds of their own plumage type rather than showing random mating behavior. It is possible that the goslings become imprinted on the plumage type of one or both of their parents shortly after hatching and later seek out a mate of the same color. If so, goslings whose parents were blue-morph would seek blue-morph mates, but those with white-morph parents would prefer typical white geese as mates. Only in cases where the young birds are the offspring of mixed parents might a gosling be imprinted on a color type opposite from its own. Dr. Cooke hypothesized that in such a case the young bird did imprint on the plumage type of one of the parents, perhaps depending on the gosling's sex. The only certain way to test this idea was to band thousands of goslings in a colony that had substantial representation of both color phases. In the late 1960s Cooke and his associates began a long-term study at La Perouse Bay to try to resolve this question. By raising captive goslings of the two color types—as well as white-morph goslings dyed pink—with foster parents that were either blue-, white-, or pink-dyed, it was possible to test the young birds' social responses when they were later placed together in a large flock. When the goslings were tested in a circular arena and allowed to move toward adults of any of the three color types, they associated predominantly with adult birds of the same plumage color as their foster parents. Even the goslings with pink foster parents responded as strongly to them as did those with normal-colored parents, suggesting that color recognition is learned rather than inherited. There was no evidence to suggest that the sex of a gosling had any effect on its behavior or that the sex of the foster parents had any effect.

The banding program undertaken by Cooke and his associates has also brought to light a number of interesting points in addition to the behavioral basis for preferential mating. First, a considerable degree of mixing of both blue- and white-morph geese from different breeding colonies apparently exists off the Gulf Coast wintering grounds, where pair formation occurs. This allows for the formation of pair bonds between birds reared in different breeding colonies. As a result, a male from one colony may form a pair bond with a female that was reared at another colony several hundred miles away. Cooke has concluded that, as is the case with ducks, it is the female rather than the male that determines to which colony the pair will return and attempt to nest. Such behavior tends to promote outbreeding between colonies, and this would also encourage genetic uniformity between breeding populations separated by several hundred miles.

The different breeding colonies in arctic Canada—those that are entirely blue-morph, white-morph, or the two types mixed in various proportions—all have different migration patterns when they head southward in the fall, and this also has important genetic and ecological implications. The predominantly blue-morph geese that breed on Baffin Island, for example, typically undertake a nearly nonstop flight to their Louisiana wintering grounds. The geese spend several weeks in early September in a staging area at James Bay, Canada, where they are subjected to fairly heavy hunting pres-

Sky sure, but their subsequent nonstop flight carries them out of reach of waterfowl hunters in the northern United States. It is only while the geese are passing the winter in Louisiana that hunters take a heavy toll on their number.

On the other hand, the predominantly white-morph geese that breed on Southampton Island and the west coast of Hudson Bay follow a more gradual and interrupted fall migration pattern. They also spend weeks along the south coast of Hudson Bay, but from there they strike out in a southwesterly direction across Ontario and southern Manitoba toward the Dakotas. In the vicinity of Devils Lake, North Dakota, and Sand Lake, South Dakota, the birds rest and take on food before continuing their flight southward. In years when the breeding season is later than usual, this stopover in the northern states is especially important, since the young of the year are unable to withstand a more direct flight to the wintering area on the coast of Texas. In such years the immature birds are especially vulnerable to hunting because of their generally weaker condition, and so up to a third of the young geese may be shot by hunters.

The genetic and ecologic implications of these differences in migratory traditions are thus substantial. Whereas the mostly blue-phase breeding population avoids heavy hunting pressure in the northern United States by its relatively non-stop migration between James Bay and the Gulf Coast of Louisiana, the predominantly white-morph populations of Southampton Island and the west coast of Hudson Bay are subjected to the effects of intensive hunting throughout their entire fall migratory route down the Great Plains to their Texas wintering areas. In addition, many sport hunters shoot the white-plumaged birds rather than darker blue-morph geese, probably because they are more conspicuous and have greater trophy appeal. Thus, the differential effects of hunting on the two plumage types supplement the differential breeding adaptations, and may influence the rate of natural selection by favoring the blue-morph genotype.

Obviously, state game agencies in the northern states have been eager to manage their temporary goose populations in a way that will assure the highest possible harvests for their hunters. Their solution has been to encourage a buildup of massive fall goose populations in a few refuge areas where the birds can safely rest. To obtain food, however, the birds must fly out beyond the refuge boundaries, where they become legal game.

Hunters in the wintering areas of Louisiana and Texas have not remained impassive in the face of increasing harvests of Snow Geese in the northern states. Both federal and state game agencies have been accused of "shortstopping" the birds in order to increase the harvests in more northerly states. This is the term applied to the management of refuges or other controlled areas along the fall migratory route by providing food or planting grain to encourage maximum fall usage by geese and to delay their departure to wintering areas for as long as possible. This procedure had its predictable outcome at various times, as when a large flock of geese and ducks that were concentrated on Lake Andes National Wildlife Refuge in southern South Dakota were affected by a severe outbreak of viral enteritis, or "duck plague," which killed thousands of waterfowl. The affected geese were Canada Geese rather than Snow Geese, but the potential for disaster of comparable or even greater magnitude certainly also exists with the highly gregarious Snow Geese.

Furthermore, many of the major nesting grounds of Snow Geese have been seriously impacted by massive population increases during the last two decades. Although the winter population of Snow Geese in the midcontinental region consisted of about a million birds in 1969, this doubled in about the next ten years. By the mid-1990s this population had ex-

Sky ceeded 3 million birds, with some estimates as high as 6 million individuals! The severe crowding effects that are now occurring during spring and fall migrations, and the disastrous vegetational degradation that has occurred on the overcrowded breeding colonies, have set the stage for greatly enhanced transmission of diseases and parasites, and the possible starvation of growing goslings. Birds at the severely overgrazed La Perouse colony, for example, have exhibited smaller average clutch sizes, reduced body sizes, and reduced gosling survival rates in recent years. Renal coccidiosis is common among goslings hatched at that colony, and often causes chick mortality. Cholera outbreaks, sometimes killing tens of thousands of birds, are now fairly common among migrants in crowded spring staging areas such as in central Nebraska, and the disease has been found in some nesting colonies as well. State and federal game agencies now believe that the midcontinent population of Snow Geese should somehow be reduced to about a million birds in order to save the breeding grounds from further degradation and reduce the probability of a massive population crash caused by one or more of these ecological dangers.

A wild goose population is thus a dynamic system that can respond rapidly and intensely to subtle and manifold environmental pressures. The Lesser Snow Goose is a prime example of the problems inherent in "managing" such a complex natural system. Additionally, the genetic "marker" provided by the blue-morph plumage variant allows a potential rare insight into the workings of natural selection in a species highly adapted to life in a harsh and intolerant environment. For better or worse, humans are influencing how selection may be affecting the genetic composition of the Hudson Bay goose flock, and human activities have greatly modified the migratory traditions of the birds as well. Each spring the Snow Geese push relentlessly northward to rendezvous with fate on distant arctic shorelines; each fall they return with the future of their species invested in a new generation of offspring produced by the most successful genetic combinations. We could ask for no greater symbol of innate determination for survival and aesthetic beauty than that provided by the Snow Geese; accordingly, we should be content with no less than a maximum commitment to their continued well-being.

Suggested Readings

The following books by P. A. Johnsgard will provide the interested reader with additional details and appropriate literature citations for the articles and essays appearing in this book.

PART I

1. *Grouse and Quails of North America.* 1973. University of Nebraska Press, Lincoln.
2. *The Grouse of the World.* 1983. University of Nebraska Press, Lincoln.
3. *The Hummingbirds of North America,* 2d ed. 1997. Smithsonian Institution Press, Washington, D.C.
4. *The Pheasants of the World.* 1986. Oxford University Press, Oxford.
5. *The Quails, Partridges and Francolins of the World.* 1988. Oxford University Press, Oxford.
6. *Bustards, Hemipodes and Sandgrouse: Birds of Dry Places.* 1991. Oxford University Press, Oxford.
7. *Arena Birds: Sexual Selection and Behavior.* 1994. Smithsonian Institution Press, Washington, D.C.

PART II

1. *Handbook of Waterfowl Behavior.* 1965. Cornell University Press, Ithaca, N.Y.

2. *Waterfowl: Their Biology and Natural History.* 1968. University of Nebraska Press, Lincoln.
3. *Waterfowl of North America.* 1975. Indiana University Press, Bloomington.
4. *Ducks, Geese and Swans of the World.* 1978. University of Nebraska Press, Lincoln.
5. *Diving Birds of North America.* 1987. University of Nebraska Press, Lincoln.
6. *Ducks in the Wild: Conserving Waterfowl and Their Habitats.* Key-Porter, Toronto (1992), and Prentice Hall, New York (1993).
7. *Ruddy Ducks and Other Stifftails: Their Behavior and Biology.* 1996. University of Oklahoma Press, Norman. (Coauthored with Montserrat Carbonell.)

PART III

1. *The Plovers, Sandpipers and Snipes of the World.* 1981. University of Nebraska Press, Lincoln.
2. *Those of the Gray Wind: The Sandhill Cranes.* 1981. St. Martin's Press, New York. Reprinted in 1987 by the University of Nebraska Press, Lincoln.
3. *The Cranes of the World.* 1983. Indiana University Press, Bloomington.
4. *The Platte: Channels in Time.* 1984. University of Nebraska Press, Lincoln.
5. *Crane Music: A Natural History of American Cranes.* 1991. Smithsonian Institution Press, Washington, D.C.
6. *Song of the North Wind: A Story of the Snow Goose.* 1974. Doubleday & Co., New York. Reprinted in 1979 by the University of Nebraska Press, Lincoln.

Citations for Previously Published Articles

Grateful acknowledgment is made to the following publications for permission to reprint the articles in this volume.

PART I

1. Introductory essay first published in the *Lincoln Journal-Star* newspaper, April 6, 1994.
2. "Dawn rendezvous on the lek." *Natural History*, March 1967, pp. 16–20. With permission from *Natural History*, © the American Museum of Natural History.
3. "The elusive tree quails of Mexico." *Animals*, November 1972, pp. 486–490.
4. "Quail music." *Natural History*, February 1974, pp. 34–39. With permission from *Natural History*, © the American Museum of Natural History.
5. "On display." *Birder's World* 3(6): 30–34.
6. "Bustards: Stalkers of the dry plains." *Zoonooz* (San Diego Zoo) 63(7): 5–11.
7. "Glittering garments of the rainbow." *Birder's World* 2(4): 12–16.

PART II

1. Essay originally published in the *Lincoln Journal-Star* newspaper, October 5, 1995.
2. "The evolution of duck courtship." *Natural History*, February

1968, pp. 58–63. With permission from *Natural History*,
© the American Museum of Natural History.

3. "The elusive musk ducks." *Natural History*, October 1965,
pp. 26–29. With permission from *Natural History*,
© the American Museum of Natural History.

4. "The ruddy duck." *Birder's World* 9(3): 48–51.

5. "Torrent ducks of the Andes." *Animals*, February 1972,
pp. 80–83.

6. "Birds of the Pribilofs." *Birder's World* 1(6): 20–23.

PART III

1. Essay originally published in the *Lincoln Journal-Star* newspaper, March 19, 1995.

2. "Flight of the sea ducks." *Natural History*, August–September
1973, pp. 68–73. With permission from *Natural History*, © the
American Museum of Natural History.

3. "The 6,000-mile odyssey of a globe-trotting bird." Reprinted
from *Wildlife Conservation Magazine*, published by the
Wildlife Conservation Society. (Originally appeared as *Animal
Kingdom*, June–July 1981, pp. 17–21.)

4. "The triumphant trumpeters." *Natural History*, November
1978, pp. 72–77. With permission from *Natural History*,
© the American Museum of Natural History.

5. "Where have all the curlews gone?" *Natural History*, August
1980, pp. 30–34. With permission from *Natural History*,
© the American Museum of Natural History.

6. "Natural and unnatural selection in a wild goose." (Retitled in
this book as "The geese from beyond the north wind.")
Natural History, December 1973, pp. 60–69. With permission
from *Natural History*, © the American Museum of Natural
History.

Index

Aleutian Islands, 102, 116, 118
Alvarez del Toro, Miguel, 24
Amazon River, 93
American Black Duck, 71
American Golden-Plover, 130–137
American White Pelican, xiv
American Wigeon, 69, 71
Anthony, H.E., 31
Arctic Fox, 102, 106, 150
Argentine Torrent Duck, 97
Attwater's Prairie-Chicken, 15
Audubon, John James, xiii, 51, 55
Australian Bustard, 41

Bach, Johann Sebastian, 112
Baffin Island, 148, 153
Banks, Richard C., 145
Bearded Tree Quail, 16–27, 31
Bechevin Bay, 117
Beebe, William, 43
Beethoven, Ludwig van, 112
Bengal Florican, 46, 48
Bent, Arthur C., 148
Bering, Vitus Jonassen, 115
Bering Sea, 101, 115
Berlin Zoo, 85
Bilstad, Hazel, xii

Birds of paradise, 6, 35
Black-bellied Plover, 133
Black-billed Magpie, xiv
Black Chachalaca, 23
Black Grouse, 6
Black-legged Kittiwake, 103–104
Blue-billed Duck, 81
Blue Goose, 148–149
Blue Grouse, 8
Blue-winged Teal, 71, 73
Bolivian Torrent Duck, 97, 98
Bornean Peacock-Pheasant, 38
Brandt, Herbert, 116, 119
Bronze-tailed Pheasant, 37
Bufflehead, 87, 91
Buffy-crowned Tree Quail, 18, 22, 23
Burchard Lake, 3

Calliope Hummingbird, 50, 57, 59
Canada Goose, 113, 155
Cape Dorset, 119
Cape Prince of Wales, 116
Cape Romanzof, 116
Caspian Tern, xiv
Cassin's Auklet, 106
Cauca Valley, 94
Cedar Point Biological Station, xiv

Chachalacas, 22
Chapin, J.P., 42
Chilean Torrent Duck, 95, 97–99
Christian Pond, 124–126
Cinnamon Teal, 71, 73, 87
Cliff Swallow, xv
Cohn, Jean, 54
Colombian Torrent Duck, 92–95
Commander Islands, 102
Common Eider, 74, 115–121
Common Goldeneye, 74, 89
Common Murre, 100, 102–105
Common Peafowl, 36, 37
Common Poorwill, xiv
Congo Peafowl, 42
Cooch, Graham, 149–151
Cooke, Fred, 151–153
Crazy Horse, 65
Crested Argus, 34, 39
Crested Auklet, 102, 106

Darwin, Charles, xvi
Davison, G., 40
Delacour, Jean, 43
Devils Lake, 154

Eared pheasants, 35
Emperor Goose, xvi
Eskimo Curlew, 138–146
European Capercaillie, 8

Falcated Duck, 69
Field Sparrow, xiv
Fisher, James, 19
Fitzpatrick, Arthur, 58
Fort Anderson, 142
Funk Island, 18
Fur Seal, 101

Gadwall, 71, 72, 87
Galveston Island, 144
Gould, John, 51, 81
Grand Teton National Park, 57, 124–129

Gray-crowned Rosy Finch, 102
Gray Peacock-Pheasant, 33, 38
Great Argus Pheasant, 33, 37, 39–42
Great Blue Heron, xi, xiv
Great Bustard, 44, 45, 47
Greater Prairie-Chicken, 2–5, 9
Greater Snow Goose, 149
Great Horned Owl, 113
Great Indian Bustard, 46
Great Lakes, 143
Great Plains, 143, 145, 146, 154
Great Slave Lake, 142
Green Peafowl, 37
Green-winged Teal, 71, 72
Gulf Coast, 141, 153
Gulf of Mexico, 136
Gulf of Saint Lawrence, 136

Heinroth, Oskar, 47
Hermit hummingbirds, 53, 54
Herring Gull, xiv
Himalayan Blood Pheasant, 35
Hooper Bay, 116, 119
Horned Guan, 23
Horned Puffin, 102, 105
Huarocondo Canyon, 96
Hudson Bay, 134, 136, 143, 148, 154, 156
Hudson's Bay Company, 140

Indian (Blue) Peafowl, 37
Izembek Bay, 117

Jackson Hole Biological Station, 59
James Bay, 145, 153
Johnson, A.W., 98

Kamchatka Peninsula, 116
King Eider, 115–121
Kortright, F.H., 89
Kuril Islands, 116
Kuskokwim Delta, 116

Lacreek National Wildlife Refuge, 128

Lake Andes National Wildlife Refuge, 155
La Perouse Bay, 151, 156
Lapland Longspur, 102, 103
Lark Sparrow, xiv
Least Auklet, 102, 106
Lena Delta, 117
Lesser Antilles, 136, 140
Lesser Florican, 46
Lesser Prairie-Chicken, 9–13
Lesser Sandhill Crane, 111–116
Lesser Snow Goose, 147–157
Little Black Bustard, 48
Little Bustard, 48
Little Curlew, 144
Long-billed Curlew, 62, 64
Long Island, 138
Long-tailed Tree Quail, 17, 22, 23
Lorenz, Konrad, 72, 77

MacFarlane, R., 142
Magdalen Islands, 141
Malayan Peacock-Pheasant, 38
Mallard, 69, 71, 72, 75–77
Manakins, 6
Manning, T.H., 149
Masked Duck, 88
Mexican Duck, 71
Migratory Bird Treaty Act, 143
Moffett, George, 95, 99
Montauk Point, 139
Mottled Duck, 71
Murphy, Robert Cushman, 138, 145
Musk Duck, 68, 78–85

National Elk Refuge, 124
National Science Foundation, 95
Niobrara River, 63
Northern Bobwhite, 29–31
Northern Fulmar, 103
Northern Pintail, 71–73, 75–77, 102
Northern Shoveler, 71, 73
Norton Sound, 117
Novaya Zemlya Archipelago, 120

Orinoco River, 93

Pacific Golden-Plover, 136
Pan American Highway, 19
Parakeet Auklet, 102, 106
Pelagic Cormorant, 103
Peruvian Torrent Duck, 95–97, 99
Peterson, Roger Tory, xvii, 19
Phillips, John C., 76
Platte River, 64
Platte Valley, 64, 111
Point Barrow, 116, 118
Point Dall, 116
Point Lay, 118
Potosí, Mount, 97
Pribilof Islands, 101–107, 137
Pribilof (Rock) Sandpiper, 102–104
Puracé, Mt., 94

Ravel, Maurice, 114
Red-faced Cormorant, 103
Red Junglefowl, 34
Red-legged Kittiwake, 102–104
Red-necked Phalarope, 102
Red Rock Lakes, 123, 124
Red Rock Lakes Migratory Refuge, 124–127
Red-winged Blackbird, xiii
Reed, Chester, xv
Reeve's Pheasant, 34
Resplendent quetzal, 23
Ridgway, Robert, 51
Ring-billed Gull, xiv
Ringed Kingfisher, 95
Ring-necked Pheasant, 34
Río Cauca, 94
Río Chisbar, 94, 95
Río de la Plata, 93
Río Grande, 94
Río Lurin, 96
Río Petrohue, 98
Río Zongo, 97
Roberts, Thomas, xiv
Rock Sandpiper, 102–104

Rockwell, Robert F., 152
Rock Wren, xiv
Roseate Spoonbill, xvi
Rothschild's Peacock-Pheasant, 38
Rowley, J.S., 23
Ruddy Duck, 66, 73, 80, 86–91
Rufous-crested Bustard, 48
Rufous Hummingbird, 58

Sage Grouse, 7, 9, 13, 47
Saint George Island, 101, 102
Saint Lawrence Island, 118
Saint Paul Island, 101, 102
Sallee, Edmund, 19
Salvadori's Duck, 98
Sandhill cranes (lesser & greater),
    111–116
Scaled Quail, 28–31
Scott, Peter, 98
Sharpe, Roger, 76
Sharp-tailed Grouse, 9–14
Sherman, William Tecumseh, xiii
Short-eared Owl, 102
Singing Quail, 24
Snow Bunting, 102, 103
Snow Goose, 147–157
Snowy Owl, 102
Soper, J. Dewey, 148
Southampton Island, 148, 154
Spectacled Eider, 115–121
Steller, G.W., 115
Steller's Eider, 115–121
Stilt Sandpiper, 136
Strait of Belle Isle, 139
Surf Scoter, 74

Sutton, George, 148
Swenk, Myron, 142

Thick-billed Murre, 102–105
Tierra del Fuego, 93, 133
Tooth-billed Hummingbird, 54
Torrent Duck, 92–99
Tragopans, 35
Trumpeter Swan, 123–129
Tufted Puffin, 102, 105
Tundra Swan, 125
Turkey Vulture, xv
Turner, L.M., 146

Urubamba River, 96
U.S. National Museum, 145

Victoria Island, 118

Warner, Dwaine, 22
Western Grebe, xiv
Western Meadowlark, 103
Whiskered Auklet, 106
Whistling Swan, 125
White-capped Dipper, 96
Whooper Swan, 125
Wildfowl Trust, 85
Williams, G.H., 144
Wilson, Loren, 63
Winter Wren, 102
Wood Duck, xvi, 87

Yellow-billed Teal, 69
Yellowstone National Park, 123
Yukon-Kuskokwim Delta, 116